TARNISHED TREASURE

TARNISHED TREASURE

How Love Captured
a Hopeless Heart

MARIA LOVELESS

TATE PUBLISHING & *Enterprises*

Published by Tate Publishing & Enterprises, LLC
127 E. Trade Center Terrace | Mustang, Oklahoma 73064 USA
1.888.361.9473 | www.tatepublishing.com

Tate Publishing is committed to excellence in the publishing industry. The company reflects the philosophy established by the founders, based on Psalm 68:11,
"The Lord gave the word and great was the company of those who published it."

Book design copyright © 2011 by Tate Publishing, LLC. All rights reserved.
Cover design by April Marciszewski
Interior design by Chelsea Womble
Author Photo by Albina Campos

Published in the United States of America

ISBN: 978-1-61777-551-2
Religion, Christian Life, Women's Issues
11.08.08

DEDICATION

First and foremost I would like to thank the One who made this book possible, and that is Jesus Christ. You are the lover of my soul, my world. You are everything to me! I would have never imagined that this is what I would have done in my life, but out of my obedience came a river of life that flowed into this book. Those whispered words that flowed out my fingers to the pages of this book are for the women who are bound in their prisons of oppression and hopelessness, and I believe these words will give them the ability to become free.

Secondly, I would like to thank Rebecca, the treasure, for trusting me to embrace her. Without her yielding her life and making it an open book to me, *Tarnished Treasure* would not have been possible. She encouraged me to believe in myself and the gifts God has given me. Because of my obedience to mentor her, in return she spent countless hours serving my family in many ways, allowing me the time to make the book become a reality. That is when I realized those who are forgiven much, love much. She has covered my family in prayer and served us with great love, devotion and loyalty. She is a covenant heart that would truly lay her life down for me. I am forever grateful.

Last but not least, a note to Jack, Lauren, and Amy, my husband and daughters. Thank you for giving me the opportunity to step into my new season. Ministering to women has been a heart's passion and calling for most of my life. By you sacrificing your wife and your mom, I was able to write *Tarnished Treasure,* and now many women will experience freedom in Christ. You are an important part of my life and heart, and I love you all very much!

TABLE OF CONTENTS

PREFACE

Tarnished Treasure is a story of a life saved by the grace of God and the unconditional love of a woman who answered the call to one who was lost.

It's a story that will touch your hearts, change your life, and deliver many from the bondage they were not aware they were in. Life can take us in various directions and situations, some good and some bad. From those bad experiences many of us have a tendency to hide hurts deep in our hearts that can render us ineffective. Even if you have been saved for many years, haven't yet found that saving knowledge and love of Jesus Christ, or are struggling to find your place in Him, this book will take you to that place of abiding peace and rest and understanding of the Father's love for you.

As you read this book, keep an open mind, and allow the Holy Spirit to start a work in you. The purpose is not to go into detail about Leah's life, but to make the connection that there are many women out there who live life as Leah did. They may be women with whom we work, speak, and are friends. We may spend time with them daily and not be aware of the bondage in that person's life or the hurts and pain they are hiding.

I am hoping that by reading this story you are able to hear God's calling and go to the same place where I had to give up self and move into what God called me to do. My calling in life isn't really to preach, teach, or to become someone famous, but to reach a world of women who are dying daily because of the bondage in their hearts and lives. It is important for us to realize that to win a hopeless woman requires sacrifice of self and unconditional love. Not judgment, only love—just unconditional love.

What I have found through this experience is that when we come to a place in our lives where we can allow the Holy Spirit to move in us and fill us with His love, we can begin to see beyond the faults, hurts, and pain of that person and move into their need.

It's called that amazing grace of God! If we can ever bring ourselves or another woman to the realization of His mercy, grace, and love, then we have accomplished what God has called us to do.

As women, we are powerful and have influence, and we are called to a dying world. Let us walk through this together and learn to live and walk in His love—the unconditional love that was able to bring a lost soul from the fire of hell into a life of clean hands and a pure heart; a realization of God's love and a life transformed.

TREASURED PIECE

I sought the Lord, and He heard me, and delivered me
from all my fears.

Psalm 34:4, NKJV

Most of us know in our minds that God knows our future and has
it all planned out. I was fifty-one and at a point where I was satisfied with the direction my life was headed. I really believed in my
heart I was doing what God had called me to do. I was a mom, a
wife, a pastor, worked in ministry and enjoyed time with my family.
There was great satisfaction in what I was doing, and I was content.
In the midst of my comfortable life, God presented a woman to
me, whom I will call Leah. I had met her occasionally in the past
exchanging vague hi's and bye's. In fact, I hate to admit it, but I
kind of tried to avoid her when I saw her because her demeanor was
rough and harsh. It's not that she was physically unattractive, but
her abrasiveness made her that way. The only reason I was speaking to her at this time was because I was a leader for a ladies' Bible
study. It was my responsibility to make everyone feel welcome and
build relationships with the women who were at my table. We were
to encourage them to stay and attend on a continual basis. The
Bible study's purpose was to get those who didn't have a personal
relationship with the Lord saved and to help women grow in the
Word of God to become free from the problems and issues of life.

Leah came to our women's Bible study only because she was invited by one of the young women from our church. It was evident she really didn't want to be there, and I wondered to myself why she came. I knew in my heart there had to be a huge reason. After many years of knowing her only as a casual acquaintance, God finally orchestrated that I sit and talk with her on a personal level. While we were engaged in a lengthy conversation, it gave me an opportunity to study her life in detail. She was very open with me about her desire not to be at this study. She voiced to me that she was Jewish and didn't want to have anything to do with church. But an hour into our conversation she divulged she was dying and doctors had given her six weeks to live. Wow! There it was! Possibly the real reason she came to this Bible study. Although there were about twenty-five other tables and other women leaders, Leah came to me. I knew at that moment this was a divine appointment, and it was my turn to step out of my box.

While she was explaining her life to me, I was deeply touched and saddened by the hurt and pain that she harbored because of life's failures. She participated in things I definitely didn't approve of, and she was addicted to alcohol, drugs, sex, and work. At that moment I realized this woman was living a lie, putting a false front that looked good from the outside, but was dark and dirty on the inside. In other words, she was a mess and no one even knew. Because of her abrasive front, everyone ran from her and no one was interested in getting to know her enough to find out she was a mess. You need to know, I wasn't necessarily seeing her as a person who held great value, nor did I feel the need to take on the job of polishing her. At this point the only thing I was sure of was that religion and the world had definitely hurt and disappointed her. I didn't know at the time just how precious her life was. The only thing I knew was that death and destruction pursued her and the pursuit of the enemy was quickly overtaking her.

At first I tried to have other ladies spend time with her, but she didn't respond to them like she did with me. For some reason she was drawn to me. Over time, I began to feel an urgency to reveal the true value in her that God created her to have. She reminded me of an old silver vase covered in tarnish that everyone ignored. I knew if I didn't bring the true value of her out, I was sure the tarnish of the world would destroy the tarnished piece.

It was revealed to me that deep inside she felt her life got to a place where it was so covered by worldly elements no one was able to see her value. Finally, because of life's failures and disappointment, she was brought to a place of despair and hopelessness and every dream she had was shattered; death knocked at her door. She was at a place of no hope and her heart cried for someone to find her and take her to a place of safety. I knew she had a longing in the middle of her desperation and I wondered to myself if her life could be delivered.

I realized the people who were supposed to care and build her up were destroying her. She lived in an abusive home; a place where no one recognized her gifting and no one saw her real value. The heart that God created to beat for Him instead filled with hurt and pain. I wondered while I listened to her what could help the pain and what could heal the hurt. She wondered to herself what would make the pain go away. It was interesting to visualize the very hands that He created to reach out to Him start to reach out to other things for answers. She thought the answers were in drugs, alcohol, and sex. Her hand continued to reach out to those things, but the hurt and pain only left momentarily. She never realized that as time went on the pain would be harder to mask and harder to hide; she continued to reach out to the things of the world for answers.

After many years of indulging in worldly things, her heart became so hardened she no longer had any understanding of love. The sin she was participating in was taking its toll. The evidence of it was manifesting in the physical body taking her to the precipice of death. During this time, her mind began to question whether death would be better than life. She knew the pain and loneliness would cease if she died and the hurt would no longer torment her mind. Deep in her heart she longed for life and hope, but could hope ever be restored to her? Could peace ever be present and could there be a place of rest?

I knew she carried a tremendous amount of bondage from her past. There were many past hurts and past pain that were masked by an abrasive front. But one day, she shared a very unique thing. She had not spoken of it to anyone afraid that they would think she was crazy. She told me that every night she would have the same dream. The dream was of a pit, a dark pit that was wet, smelled moldy, and also smelled of smoke and fire. There were chains that clanged and hung from the wet dark walls, and there was this laughter that wasn't from joy, but a taunting laugh that heckled to the point of craziness. There were demons that chased after her and caught her and would hold her down on a cement slab. She said there was a man—she called him Satan—who stood at the end of the cement slab near her head. The demons would continue to hold her down, and Satan would laugh and say things like, "You'll always be mine. You will never be able to escape me or my demons. I have placed them with you, and they will always be with you. You gave up your life to me long ago, and you're mine!" She told me the same dreams had been going on every night for more than twenty-seven years.

Some time passed after our initial conversation and then she told me that she had a different dream. This time it was a dream of being transported to a corporate office in a high-rise building. She had been escorted into this office, and the room glowed. There was a big desk and a big chair that was turned facing toward the window. When she approached the desk, the chair turned; there was a man sitting and His face shone brightly. He stood up and said nothing. Then He walked toward her and held His hand out and said, "Trust me. Trust me. Will you trust me? I want you to take my hand and dance with me." The one thing she noticed was that this man was a gentleman, one whom she had never encountered before. She felt a peace and a comfort that was unexplainable. He left the choice up to her. She could take His hand and dance, or she could walk away like she always had before. She was not very trusting and wanted to keep her heart from feeling any more hurt and pain, so in her dream, she backed away.

I spent many days and nights trying to answer her questions while building a sense of trust. I decided that it was time to get her to understand the necessity of turning her life over to the One who wanted to dance with her. It was a long process and I knew I had to take my time, but I knew she was dying. She told me life didn't matter anymore because she was going to die anyway. That statement penetrated to the core of my heart. I lost my mother to cancer three years prior to meeting Leah and I was bound and determined that Satan was not going to take anyone else from me by cancer or illness. Aside from that fact, I knew she needed someone to love her and appreciate her for who she was. When I met her I found a very cold, hard-hearted individual who had lost the will to fight for life. I knew hopelessness was setting in, and I wanted to grab hold of her before it took her to her death. It was a battle she couldn't fight alone, and I needed to step in and guide her to life, a life I knew she had never before known. I needed to pose to her that she needed the Lord, and that only He would be able to fill the emptiness and heal the hurt and pain she had hidden for years.

During the course of the women's Bible study, she always got up from the table and left during worship. I decided it was time to pose the concept of salvation to her. So when she got up to leave I left my table and followed her. When I caught up with her and asked why she walks out she said "it" made her feel uncomfortable. There was my opening! I explained that feeling was the Lord drawing her to Him.

I told her right out, "You need the Lord."

She said, "No, I don't."

Immediately I was curious as to why she would say this.

She answered, "He doesn't love me."

My eyes filled with tears, I responded, "Oh, yes He does, and so do I."

At that moment I knew Leah desired to be loved, but felt no one ever did. That was the key to her heart. Love, unconditional love, the only kind of love the Father can give. I knew she had no idea what being loved was truly about. Her relationship with her natural father was difficult and filled with anything but love, and she knew that people kept their distance from her, so she knew they didn't love her either. That was my key to her heart and an opening that was a mile wide for me to walk through.

After that moment I knew she wasn't very receptive to this proposed truth and finding Him, and I knew that I had to ask God for her life. I knew I needed to intercede on her behalf and ask God to be merciful and extend her life until she could realize she really needed Him. This time it wasn't about the fact that she was dying from cancer; she was dying inside from all of the exposure of the weight and hurts of the world. The world had taken its toll on her heart and her life. She had lived selfishly and now I needed her to apply the same passion to seeking the One who could give her life and who could heal all the hurts and wounds of her past. So my job at this point was to show her love, a love that she had never before experienced in her life. I knew at that moment that all I could do was listen and not judge her or her life. I needed to be an open book to her and offer to be there at any time.

I left with my family on vacation, and left her my number in case she felt she needed to talk or needed anything at all. I was annoyed to find out that she had never had that extended to her, and she was very intrigued with that extension of kindness. She was battling with health issues, she spent time in the hospital, but mostly she was feeling lost and alone, and hopelessness was setting in fast. One night she blurted out that she had a desire to end her life and just "get it over with." She further explained that after I told her God loved her, and I loved her, that there was a small place deep in her heart that still felt something. What if what I had told her was true? What if there was a God that could love and give you a life with peace and security? What if He could give her a second chance at life and it could be different? She told me all of these things were running through her head, as she laid reeling from the pain of the cancer. My perception was the pain of the cancer wasn't even close to the pain that she had hid in her heart for so many years.

Amazingly enough, Leah started to reach out to me. She started asking questions. Her questions were intelligent and seeking truth. I felt this was good, because if she was curious enough to ask questions, then there was still a little life left in her. I realized that she was seeking truth and that she desired to understand everything God had for her. I wanted to explain to her that she just needed to grab hold of God and have faith that He would do what He said He could do. But how could I tell her that? I came home from vacation, and I immediately went to see her. God spoke to me; I knew that if I didn't get her to pray and accept Jesus as her personal Savior, she would die and would live eternally in that pit that she had dreamed about for many years. I sat down next to her, and I could see the physical toll the illness was taking on her. More than that I could feel the pain and hurt and knew it was time to introduce her to the One who desired to dance with her. I reached out my hand and asked her to place her hand in mine. I asked her to pray with me, but before she did she made the proclamation that a major transformation and deliverance from her past would have to happen or it wouldn't be worth it. She said if that couldn't happen and she couldn't experience deliverance, then the destruction that was in front of her would take her. I told her it was time, and that night I prayed with her and introduced her to a new life. It was a life that God had desired for her for many years.

The tarnished piece moved immediately from darkness to light and became a new creature in Christ. Her conversion was pretty amazing. Initially, it was the ability to trust me; for her to hold out her hand when asked was a major step in the right direction. When

I prayed with her, I knew that it definitely touched the depths of her heart. Immediately, I saw the Spirit of God start to pierce through the wall that had protected her heart for so many years. Ever since she moved her life into the light, the darkness would tempt and try to pull her back while making promises it could not hold. The darkness lied saying her past life was easier and better. It called for her to return to them daily. What was worse was the pain of the past tried to torment her, and the temptation to mask it with the vices she used in the past was very seductive.

I realized at this point that I needed to totally submerse and saturate her in the kingdom of light. It was essential to her survival. She found a place that felt safe, a place where there was peace she had never known, a place that she knew the darkness of her past could not penetrate. I decided to open the doors of our home to her. After I made this decision, trust me, I received much resistance from outsiders because of the type of life Leah had led. But I knew that if I didn't provide a safe place away from the vices of her past, the darkness that she had walked in for so many years would draw her back because it was familiar to her. I needed to put her in a place where I could seclude her and teach her and submerse her into a new life. I knew at this point she didn't fully trust God. I knew she had reached out her hand to dance but hadn't quite allowed Him to embrace her. Leah asked, "How could you allow someone to embrace you whom you could not see and could not touch?" Leah learned that in order to survive in life she couldn't trust anyone. She asked me, "How can someone trust?" I knew trust was a big issue for her, and it was something with which we were going to have to deal. I knew she had started to trust me, but I didn't want to delude myself into thinking that she fully trusted me either. It was interesting for me to see and learn that people who have experienced such hurt and pain in their lives start to literally recede from life. We are really created to commune with people, and if we can't trust them, then we are unable to commune with them. This was an issue that was sure to come to light, and I waited for that moment where we could address trust.

One day soon after she was saved, we were standing in church and the people there were worshiping with their hands lifted high. I saw her looking around, and she leaned over and asked me why people lifted their hands during worship. I explained it in a way I knew she would understand, and that was comparing it to when the police tell someone to surrender. I asked her, "What do you do?"

She told me, thinking back to parts of her past, she understood that a sign of surrender is lifting your arms in the air. It is a time when we display that it is no longer our will, but are at the will of the one who demands our surrender. She told me there were many times in her life that she was at a place of forced surrender in the presence of people who placed no value on her life and many who abused her.

She was learning that raising the arms and yielding the heart are a cry for freedom from the bondage of her heart. I could take her to that place of submission, but only she could open the hidden places of her heart to the man in her dream who said, "Trust me," and called her to "dance with Him." I could see her heart yearned and longed for freedom. The gripping chains of the past weighed heavy on her heart, and I knew it was freedom or death for her. Freedom cried for the chains to be loosed, and there was only one person who had the power to break those chains—the One whom she is learning to trust, love, and to completely surrender her life.

After being involved in ministry for many years, I realized we need to know what our true goal really is. No matter what we think people have or need, our job should always be to ask if they truly have a relationship with Christ. We can plant seeds, we can preach to them about their actions and sin, but what we really need to be is an example of God's love and affection. That is what it will take for the lost to realize what God truly has for them. If I had preached, I would have only chased her off, and the end result would have brought her death physically and spiritually.

I know now that our primary purpose is to relay to the lost His love. We can't place our focus on the sin in their life or on their past because after they accept Him they will have a desire to live a clean life and purity will follow. The surprising thing for me to realize was Leah didn't really believe God could forgive her for her past sin. Her life was so compromised and saturated by the world that her heart had become hardened by many years of living that way. My sole purpose was to lead her to the saving knowledge of the Lord, by being that example of love to her, a love she had never known in her life. I needed to be a constant source of strength to her in the wake of battle. I knew I needed to start building a trust with her so she could possibly see that God would always love her no matter what she had done.

We are to become that sweet fragrance to a lost and dying world, and a true example of Christ. We need to pray that our sweet aroma will fill their lives and melt the walls of the hardened hearts of the lost. Are you willing to step out of your comfortable life and become the sweet aroma of Christ and stop looking at the sin and see the sinner?

HIDDEN VALUE

Behold, You desire truth in the inner being; make me to
know wisdom in my inmost heart.

Psalm 51:6, AMP

Picture a very rare, precious, and valuable piece of silver. Only the
maker of the piece knows its true value, and there is no other piece
that has ever been made like it. It is one of a kind. Every detail of
the piece was pre-planned. The piece of art was crafted, shined,
polished, and sold as a high-priced, valuable piece of art.

Over time the new owner of the piece did not appreciate the
value of the expensive piece of art as the creator did. The piece
had been uncared for and neglected. As time went by, the piece of
art gave the appearance of having no value because it became tarnished. The shine was gone because it became covered with worldly
matter. Eventually, the piece was viewed as having no great value.
People would see it day in and day out, and no one recognized the
one of a kind piece of art and the true value it held.

In crafting an art piece, there is a molding process that has to
happen. When the artist molds the piece, it is of an image he holds
in his mind. Just like the art piece is created in the natural, we too
are individually handcrafted and created as a unique masterpiece of
God. No two people are alike, and no two people are made with the
same DNA or fingerprints. God the curator created you like no one
else; you are unique and individual.

Listen to what our Creator says about us, His pieces of art. He has formed our inward parts and knows every fiber of our being. The Bible tells us we are fearfully and wonderfully made. Do any of us really understand what that means? It means that we are a marvelous piece of artwork. Before we were born, God knew every intricate detail in how He made us. We are skillfully made by His hands. God saw our substance, even before we were formed. Even at that time, though the days of our life hadn't occurred yet, God had them all planned out.

When the artist is finished creating his piece of art, he delights in it, and that is how God sees us—His thoughts are precious toward us. If God's thoughts could be counted they would be more in number than the sand of the sea. The union of the egg and sperm really wasn't where we began; we began in the mind of God. All of us are fearfully and wonderfully made by Him.

All of us are born into a world that is full of elements that can destroy. It is not always our decision and will as to what we are exposed; nevertheless, when we are exposed to the elements of the world, the destruction process begins. Sin, which is a worldly element, is something that causes us to be separated from God like it did with Adam and Eve. When we choose to indulge in the things of the world and we reject Christ, our communion with Him is severed. Regardless of that separation, the Creator always pursues to place our lives back into His hands. His desire is to walk with us and reveal our true value to us.

God tells us there is no forgiveness of sin without a sacrifice. When Adam and Eve sinned, God in His loving mercy sacrificed an innocent animal to provide a covering for them. He removed them from the garden, the place of temptation, so they would not eat of the tree of life and live forever in their sin. His mercy provided a place of protection for them and prevented them from getting what they really deserved. Even today His mercy protects and prevents us from getting what we really deserve because of the sin to which we expose ourselves.

God had a plan before He created Adam and Eve, just like God has a plan for us knowing that we have the same weaknesses and desires as they did. At the time of Adam and Eve very few were allowed to commune with God. But, His initial desire was for all to commune with Him. That means His desire is for you and I to commune with Him, too. God had a greater plan than just covering the sin. He had a plan that would pay the price for all sin, no longer just to cover the sin, but to remove sin once and for all. In the Bible it tells us the perfect Lamb was slain before the foundation of the world. God not only handcrafted us before we were in our mother's womb, but He had a plan to remove all the sin of the world from our lives. God's plan was that He would send His Son, Jesus Christ, to be born of a woman, walk the earth as a perfect man, and be sacrificed as the perfect Lamb, shedding His blood for the forgiveness of all of our sins. No longer would our sin just be covered, but He actually saved us from the consequences of that sin. The end result of salvation is He released us from our sordid past and set us free. You can compare it to someone committing a crime and the judge giving a sentence of prison, money, or parole. Then imagine an innocent person approaching the perpetrator and saying, "I will serve your time in prison, pay all your fines, and serve your parole time." The person who committed the crime walks out owing and being bound by nothing. That's what God did when He sent Christ to shed His blood for us. He paid the price for every one of our sins, freeing us from every debt we owe. That is God's mercy.

When the sins of our past are brought to light, we have the assurance that Jesus Christ is more than sufficient to remove any tarnish of our past. Leah can now be declared a pure vessel because the blood of Jesus paid the price for her sins. Her past has been paid for, but the remnants from her worldly exposures still remain. I realized the process of cleansing required a greater hope being imbedded in her heart. I had to show her there was something greater than the eyes of her heart had ever seen. Hope in her heart would be all that prevails over the tantalizing portraits her past had painted in the recesses of her mind. The promise that was made to her was thoughts of peace, not of evil, to deliver her to a future and a hope. How could I get truth to overcome and prevail? Could the promise of what her future held for her outweigh the disappointments of her past?

I knew the ear-gate of the heart had to be protected from the accuser's tongue. Satan is the one who torments and whose whole focus is to steal our lives. Those who know the evils of her past and only see her past believe there is no hope of future transformation. Most of them have grown up in the confines of religion and forget that we are all destined for hell without Jesus Christ. We must remember that God does not hold a measuring stick against sin. The religious seem to forget hell places no price on man, and Jesus paid the same price for all. There are constant reminders as the sins of the past come to light that God's love can reach beyond the superficial feeling that man calls love. Unconditional love does not count a person's sins against them. In fact, it covers and protects us from the world. Love assists God in the refining and cleansing process by speaking truth in love, but never judging. We must never forget the power of God's love has delivered us all from the pits of hell. There is no sin that is too great or too small. Sin is sin. Those who are forgiven much love much. Regardless of our past, my desire is that we may all recognize that we have been forgiven much.

Most of us are aware that famous and very expensive pieces of art are the greatest value in their original form. If they are altered or changed, it diminishes their value. Today, we live in a society that promotes altering and accepts sin of any sort. If we allow the valued pieces, which God created to continue in their tarnished state, then we are allowing Satan to devalue and destroy who we were originally created to be. We cannot hide or walk away from those who are lost and living a compromised life. It is up to us to find those lost treasures and lead them to the place where God can clean them and change them so they can walk in the plan and purpose God has ordained.

We must see beyond the darkness that covers people's lives and recognize the true value within them. Love covers a multitude of sin. Love covers and never exposes, and it also penetrates the barriers of the heart that conceal the true value in us. Love reminds us of the cleansing power of the blood of Jesus. Love speaks truth of a future and hope while allowing the love of God to gradually penetrate the heart. Love declares life and not death and allows conviction to draw us to repentance and rejects condemnation at all cost. Love is never failing and speaks truth and life. Love encourages us to keep our eyes fixed on the future—a future of peace and hope—and discourages us from looking back to our past. Love pursues restoration for the one person who has lost much.

THE HEART

Would not God have discovered it, since He knows the
secrets of the heart?

Psalm 44:21, NIV

Things that we touch and feel are tangible. However, those things
do not define man; what is in man's heart does. Most of us have
decided to hide who we really are and bury every dark secret in our
hearts. We have disguised the heart by covering it with false images.
If we can make ourselves look good enough, or in some instances
crazy enough, then the heart can be protected because of what we
are hiding in it. Some women mask their hearts by dressing their
bodies to fit into what society deems acceptable, and some blatantly
defy the standard of society by dressing in a creative fashion or
doing creative things. The reason people do these things is to be
rejected by others and set apart. In both instances they are protecting their heart from exposure.

One day, I wondered if others battle with the same things as
I do. When I look at myself in the mirror and see things I am
unhappy with or ashamed of, I wonder if any of us can stand naked
before a mirror and not find any flaws. Can any of us reflect on our
actions for the day and not regret something we said or did? Can
we look at our past and remember a time when we betrayed a friend
or were betrayed by one? We can always find fault with others and
ourselves. What if there was a place of no fault and we could find it?

What if there was a place where everything that was hidden could be exposed and not judged? Some of the things we keep hidden are evil thoughts, evil acts, and deceit of the heart. The very thought of that place brings fear of rejection, shame, mockery, and guilt to many. We hide and camouflage ourselves so well that no one can know how inadequate we are or how evil our heart really is. If people knew the things we hide in our heart, many of us would be left alone and forgotten.

When we hide our hearts, there is a false sense of security in that. We think if we can mask and camouflage ourselves with expensive attire to hide our bodies then surely no one will know our heart and the things we've hidden in it. What are some things that can change the condition of the heart? What is true love? There is a true love, a pure love the world does not know or understand. It allows us to stand naked physically and emotionally with no judgment, guilt, shame, rejection, or mockery. It's a love that is never moved by our imperfections or inadequacies. It's a love that always accepts and never rejects. It's a love none of us have ever known until we have met the Savior, the one true love. It's the one love that can break every barrier, wall and every hurt and pain that we have brought on ourselves by loving the things of the world. The world thinks they know or understand what true love is, but they never really grasp that true understanding. Love is not things. It's not something that is tangible or that we can feel. Only true love can release the prisoner from the bondage of their heart and never judges, taunts, or rejects. It's a love that can literally transport and transform a dying soul and bring life and hope to it. It can bring light to a dark life and a future to anyone who thought they had no reason to live. It's a pure, undefiled love that is there waiting to hold the hopeless, purify the heart, and transport you to a place of complete peace and rest.

When I was growing up, I was always picked last for anything pertaining to sports. I was the worst of the worst. When God dealt out athletic ability, He obviously forgot about me! We live in a society that makes choices according to what our senses tell us. We make decisions on what pleases the eye, what feels good, what tastes good, what sounds good, and what smells good to us. Nobody ever chooses someone by what they think is in their heart. When we choose someone for a game, a job, or our life mate, generally the first thing we choose them by is their outer appearance or if we are attracted to them—definitely not by the condition of their heart. If we would choose our friends, mates, and employees by the condition of their heart, most of the time we would be better off. It's difficult to make decisions based on a person's heart when we first meet them because we can't know or understand their heart until they reveal to us the things that are hidden in it.

Many of my life experiences have convinced me the heart is where we harbor our feelings that feed our desires. It takes years of influences from our parents, teachers, mentors, friends, and family to mold us into a certain pattern of thinking. But as we grow older, we start to establish our own patterns of thinking. We start to shove away the things people taught us growing up and lean on the desires of our own heart for making decisions. At that point of independence, we begin to realize that we can make our own decisions and listen to the desires that are in our own minds and hearts. We do the things that we desire to do and reject that still, small voice that speaks to us deep inside. Each of us was created with a still, small voice that is our God-directed conscience. Whether we are saved or not, we still possess that still, small voice that tries to direct us and keep us from danger. Most of the time, we ignore that small voice and do what is pleasing and desirable to us.

Leah experienced many things in life that I have never been exposed to myself. I have lived a sheltered life, and most of it was in church. It was interesting for me to see the difference in the thought process of someone who spent many years living a worldly life, exposed to worldly things. Even though she is not a child physically, she is a baby spiritually, and her patterns of thinking and thought processes have to be retrained. It is not just children who need to have their thought processes trained. When we become new creatures in Christ we are like little children, and our thoughts need to be retrained and renewed.

Our bodies stay physically the same. We still desire what is pleasing to our eyes, what feels good, etc. It is those outside influences that start to pick away at our hearts. Years of abuse, for instance, can tear at the heart and create an oppression that is hard to escape. That oppression penetrates to the core of the heart and places walls around it and starts to mold it into a person whom we were not created to be. When the heart starts to harden, it loses its sensitivity to the people and things around it. The heart becomes hardened to the things in life that it was created to care about. Leah had many years of abuse and outside influences that tore at her heart and oppressed her and kept her in bondage for years. This caused a hardness of the heart that was virtually impossible to penetrate without God's intervention.

When we live a life that is not pleasing to God and decide to walk our own path, we open ourselves up to worldly impressions. Originally our hearts were created for us to seek the things of God, to desire the purpose and plan that He created us to do. His plan was for us to seek out only Him. We are to deny our desires, deny the ugly things of the world that can harden our hearts. If we don't deny these things, we can become immune to the things of God.

Satan's motivation is to bombard us with these worldly pleasures. The more worldly the pleasures we indulge in, the further away we get from fulfilling the plan and purpose of the heart. Walls go up, hurts and pain are hidden, and things are done to mask the hopelessness we begin to feel. Once Satan puts us in a place of hopelessness, our spirit man diminishes and oppression will set in. We get to a place where we are truly desperate, but have no sense of where to search to find answers.

There is a place where we can search to find answers, and it is in that still, small voice inside us. It is the voice of the Spirit of God drawing us, but it is our openness to that drawing from the Spirit that causes our faith to rise in us. When faith is available, there is the smallest amount of hope that arises because God is waiting for us to answer the call. He can fill the emptiness with a purpose; He can break down the walls of a hardened heart and can turn a heart to love again by placing within us a desire to please only Him. The love of the Father is the conqueror of all hardened hearts.

My desire is that you will allow Him to tear those walls down that have been built up for you to survive the ugliness of the world. You will need to completely remove yourselves from the desires that will lead you to stray into Satan's territory. Don't get to the place of hopelessness and become immune to the call and things of God and unable to hear that still, small voice. There is no heart that is too hardened for Him to be able to soften to the things of God. Leave the life of worldliness, and allow God to penetrate the heart that He created to beat and desire Him. Allow the conqueror of hardened hearts to hold and mold yours into a life that will love at all costs.

STONES OF JUDGMENT

However, when they persisted with their questions, He raised Himself up and said, "Let him who are without sin among you be the first to throw a stone at her."

John 8:7, AMP

The more time you spend with someone, the more intimate the relationship can become. Over time, love and affection grows for them. When we think of intimate relationships, some of us may think back to some of our past relationships where intimacy didn't foster love. The interesting thing is that if we commune with God—maybe in prayer, quiet time, or time in the Word—it will foster an intimacy, and His love will be revealed to us. Many of us need to know God is not like some of the relationships we have known—the ones that promise love, but deliver abuse or say they want to offer us love only to deliver sex. Just like the time spent with someone you love, time spent with God reveals His character and goodness. God is love, and intimacy with Him develops a relationship with a longing desire and passion to spend more time with Him.

It is intimacy and the development of a friendship that is based on pure love, so much so that our hearts become consumed with Him. Our love for Him becomes stronger than a superficial love for the things of the world. The longing to commune with our Creator becomes stronger than the desire for the things that superficially satisfy us. If a person has a lover and he is ignored, he will soon leave and seek intimacy with someone else. As our intimacy increases with God and the lovers of the past are ignored, those lovers will flee to find another.

Phileo love is a touchy-feely love based on physical and superficial satisfaction. An example of superficial satisfaction is the lust and love we have for vices, such as sex and food. These are things that satisfy our physical desires, our flesh. *Agape* love is a pure love, the God kind of love, and it is based on purity. God's love will never defile, never betray, never use, and never abuse. God longs to be the love of our lives, the lover of our soul. Many of us often place the tangible things of the world above our true lover. These things are things that will hold no value someday because they are meaningless. God longs for our hearts to be sold out to Him. When we commune with the One who so lovingly created us then our love for tangible things decreases, and the longing for communion with Him will increase.

When love is applied, it covers the sin and destroys the barriers that block the heart, and then hope can be imparted, bringing a future that signals a "call" for us to live. A weary soldier can become strengthened when he fixes his eyes on the hope of his future. There is a higher calling that beckons us to a life of purpose, and when that is implanted in our hearts, our past slowly dissipates. The locks will be removed, and the chains of bondage will fall off one by one because the love of God always prevails.

A story in the Bible that I love is of an adulterous woman who was brought to Jesus by some religious hierarchy. The religious people caught her in the very act of adultery. The law at that time commanded that committing such a sin the person should be stoned to death. Jesus was there, and immediately He responded to the accusers. He didn't address the adulterous woman first. He addressed the religious hierarchy, inviting those who were without sin to cast the first stone.

Religion is very different from a relationship with God. A relationship with Him offers freedom and deliverance from the chains of bondage and the captivity of our prisons. Religion points fingers and accuses, but offers no freedom or solution. Religion condemns and requires the person pay the penalty for their sin and casts the stones of judgment. Relationship convicts and reminds us that Jesus Christ paid the penalty of sin and opens the prison doors for us and gives us freedom and deliverance for the captive.

The religious people who stood in front of Jesus and accused the woman of sin departed from their presence one by one. They were convicted by their conscience, and no religious accusers were left—only Jesus and the woman. The mouths of the accusers were silenced by the man who offered her a relationship with love and a promise of freedom. The Messiah who came to set the captives free told her, "I don't condemn you, go and sin no more."

The adulterous woman had fallen into the arms of defiled love, but when she stood in the presence of the man, Jesus, He gave her permission to walk free from the captivity of her past. Leah stood in the presence of that same man, and He has given her permission to walk free from the captivity of her past. Her accusers stand and point at her past, casting stones of judgment, but the One who came to set the captive free unlocked the chains of bondage and opened the prison door saying, "I do not condemn you, go and sin no more."

You see, we can be like the religious and cast stones of judgment against those that have a sordid past, or we can choose to stand in relationship with Him and cast love and forgiveness. We can offer the unbeliever hope for a future when all they had was a life of hopelessness. Unconditional love is difficult at best when you deal with the actions of someone's past, but the rewards are great, for we are given a gift of blessings that we would have never reaped. One of the blessings we receive is that we are able to love unconditionally without casting judgment because in Him there is no condemnation, and if we walk in *agape* love, we walk according to His purpose and plan.

FRIENDS

This is what the Lord says: "Cursed is the one who trusts in man, who depends on flesh for his strength and whose heart turns away from the Lord."

Jeremiah 17:5, NIV

Leah lived a life of independence and self-satisfaction. She was tainted by the things of the world, but had been forgiven and changed. Before her life was changed, every life decision she made was based on her past experiences. If someone is abused as a child, the experience can cause life decisions to be made based on fear or a lack of trust. It teaches them to protect and hide their heart from further abuse. A life spent searching and full of bad decisions was what led Leah to try and find protection, love and contentment. Leah always lived life to the fullest and dreamt that out there was something else that was bigger and better than the life she was living. Even with all of that type of worldly fun and living, she wandered through life realizing there was no hope and all of it was just a dream.

What are safety, protection, love, satisfaction, pleasure, contentment, success, and hope? Where are they to be found, and is there really such a thing as hope?

The life she lived was very hard and difficult. Leah realized as a small child that no one would ever be there for her, so she was pretty much on her own. She had a mother who had experienced quite a bit of illness, a father who was distant at best and who didn't know how to love, but only knew how to criticize. She had one saving grace, and that was her paternal grandmother, whom she trusted and loved more than anyone in her life. Leah pretty much raised herself and sought comfort and safety in her grandmother. Her grandmother was someone she could talk to about anything and she knew that she would still be loved. One day the family moved away to a different city, and she compared it to hell. It was two and a half hours away from the safety and security of her grandmother. Tensions ran high at home with her dad, and the physical and verbal abuse continued to get worse and worse. There was constant picking and demeaning, and nothing she did was good enough to satisfy her father. He was a perfectionist, thinking that if he pushed and pushed it would make her pursue greatness. She was naturally talented athletically and academically, but because she could never please her father, there set in a lack of desire to complete schoolwork. The sports never suffered, but her anger and attitude began to change. He was the type of father who would criticize from the bench at her sporting events in front of other fans, embarrassing her. The constant harassment caused her to feel that she wasn't loved or wanted and Leah started to seek out fulfillment in other avenues.

Drinking and drugs were readily available, and no one knew, no one even noticed. Leah was able to handle the constant threats at home and shrug off the abuse, knowing that she could handle it because she didn't even feel anymore. Little did she know that by indulging those forces she was setting herself up for destruction. Leah learned not to trust and grew up feeling that no one loved her. She became hard to handle and difficult to be around. She had anger issues and constant fights and she wouldn't take direction from her authority figures. Finally, Leah left home and was told to never return.

We all live in a world that is very real and tangible, meaning that we can touch and feel things. We need to know our five senses are what lead and drive us. We know what we like to see and know what is pleasant to our eyes and what our heart desires. We know those things that are pleasant to our ears such as our favorite music and words that bring comfort. We have favorite smells, many of them that bring to mind pleasant memories of our favorite foods. All of us continue to pursue that which is pleasant to our senses. The flesh, our physical bodies, at times can speak very loudly to us. It doesn't speak audibly, but when we desire or crave something, we sure know what it wants.

When my youngest daughter was two years old, we would eat out once a week at our favorite Mexican restaurant. After dinner a couple of times, we bought her a peppermint patty candy. She loved the taste of that candy, and after a few times, she craved and expected to get the candy each time we went. We told her she couldn't have the candy one evening, and our sweet little two-year-old turned into a tantrum-throwing child. Her flesh and everything in her let us know she really wanted and desired that candy. Everyone in that restaurant would have thought we had beaten her. When we are denied the satisfaction of something we want to see, hear, taste, touch, or smell, we don't hold back our feelings in response to being denied the pleasure. Our life is spent in pursuit of fulfilling our flesh.

Aside from our flesh we have our mind, will, and emotions. Our minds are what process all the information, whether we like what we see, hear, taste, smell, or touch. My daughter tasted the candy, and her mind decided it was good and pleasant. Her will made the decision that she liked it, and if she didn't get it, she would make sure we knew what her desires were. Our mind, will, and emotions are considered our soul. If our soul is stronger than our flesh, it will actually control it. That is one of the reasons we correct our children. As parents we are training the child to be directed and guided by their mind, will, and emotions rather than listening to the demands of their flesh. In the growing and training process they learn moral standards to gauge and determine the decision-making process so there is some control in their lives. The flesh with the five senses, if left alone, will lead to trouble. You see, if we go after everything that is pleasing to us and we satisfy our senses, then it will lead us to things that will destroy us. If I ate everything that my senses desired, I would be extremely overweight.

I want to present three different women with very different personalities and characters. All are very close friends and hang out with each other all the time. Friend number one has a zeal and zest for life. She desires to live life to the fullest and is very boisterous. She will try anything and everything at least once, and, of course, if it feels good, why stop? Her motto is "if it feels good, do it." Her greatest interest is pleasing herself, and it's always "me, me, me."

Friend number two is just happy to hang out with her friends. She doesn't really like to make decisions and would prefer not to. She will pretty much follow her friends anywhere, and that depends on which friend is the most persuasive. Friend number three is pretty quiet. Doesn't believe in the motto "if it feels good do it," and her concern is for the welfare and well-being of her other two friends. She will go along if the others decide to do something even if it's against her wishes, just to make sure they stay out of trouble. She will give her opinion, but it is often ignored, especially if friend number two sides with friend number one.

These three friends, being very different, pull against each other's desires. Do you ever feel at times when you have to make decisions concerning your own life that inside you have these three friends? That's because in reality you do. Let's take a look at the three friends we have in ourselves. The first friend is your flesh. Your flesh is only out for itself. Running after whatever looks good, feels good, tastes good, sounds good, and smells good with no concern for the consequences. There is no stopping it if the desire for fulfillment is there, and if it feels good it will just keep on doing it no matter whom it may hurt. It's all about self and the more the flesh desires something the louder it gets until it gets its way. The second friend is like your soul. Within your soul are your mind, will, and emotions. Your mind is your thinker. It's responsible for processing the decisions you make in life. Your will makes those decisions, and your emotional response follows. Your soul will follow the friend that is the most persuasive. If the flesh, friend number one, yells loud enough and is persuasive enough, then the soul will follow the flesh. They will buddy up and run off to do things with friend number three following behind. The third is the spirit man. The spirit man is where the conscience of man dwells. The spirit man desires to do what is best for the soul and the flesh. It is not just concerned about itself, but for the better interest of the others, the flesh and the soul. The spirit of man does not yell, but offers quiet direction, guidance, counsel, and is that still, small voice. You know! The one that speaks to us, and most of the time we ignore?

The more we feed the desires of our flesh, the more it gets away with, and the more it craves. Did you ever have a friend who knew how to manipulate and persuade and always lead the group? That is the goal of the flesh, and it will get as loud as it needs to get its way. As long as the flesh can persuade the soul that holds the mind, will, and emotions, then it will have its way.

In our lives, our goal should be that the spirit man would always rule and reign as king in our lives. It should guide our every decision and walk in life. The soul should be the servant. The servant submits to the king and follows orders. The flesh should be the slave, only following the orders made by the king or the spirit man. There will always be a constant battle between the three parts of man. The flesh thinks nothing of the spirit when persuaded to act. As long as it can get the soul on its side, it's happy and will always do as it pleases.

We are all created as *Spirit Beings*. God is Spirit and created us in His image and likeness. In order for man to commune with Him as He desires, He had to make us the same as He is, a spirit being. The physical body is just a shell that we occupy while living on earth. While living here, God is a jealous God and wants to commune with us. Our physical bodies can't fly up to the heavens whenever we want to talk to God, so that is why we have our spirit man. Our spirits are allowed to speak and hear what God is telling us. Unfortunately, we have the other two friends as well, and most of the time they are louder than our spirit man. We can drown out God so easily and miss His voice, and that will lead us in a different direction than what He originally desired for us.

When we go through life and continue to feed our flesh and soul and live a life as Leah did, then we are excommunicating God. In essence we are acting on our own behalf, and because we have diminished our spirit man, then we are leading and guiding our own lives. That is not living the life that God intended for us to live. His sole purpose was to create us so that we can walk and talk with Him constantly. It is His desire to commune, speak, talk, and lead us to our successes in life. If we suppress the spirit man, then we suppress what God has for us in our lives. We lose the meaning and purpose of our life and walk a path of self-destruction.

Many of us may have been raised to know what is right and wrong, and none of us were raised without any moral instruction. Without the Spirit of God living in us to guide and direct us in our decision-making process, then life becomes somewhat of a gamble. Temptation can start with a small thing, such as a favorite food that we give into, growing into bigger desires such as illicit sex, drinking, and other things the world has to offer us. The more we feed the flesh, the less we feed our spirit man, the less we can communicate and hear God. That is what Leah did. She desired to feed her flesh more than she wanted to feed her spirit man. Pretty soon her flesh took over, and it got whatever it desired. There was no room for the spirit man in her; she walked and talked the world, and it became the king in her life, so it ruled and reigned over her. Because her life was so entwined with the world, she couldn't hear God or the things of the spirit. Her flesh ruled her life and led her on a path of self-destruction. Even though the Spirit of

God was trying to reach and draw her, her flesh was so loud it diminished the calling within her from her spirit man.

It is important for us to realize what the struggles are in us and what happens when we pay attention to one friend more than the other. When we come to Christ, the spirit of man is made new, and it comes alive in us. At that point we need to start feeding and paying attention to the part of us that just came alive, or it will start to retreat. Just like when we are babies, if we aren't fed, then we won't grow and mature, and we die.

Before we are saved, the Spirit of God pulls and tugs on our spirit man. He begins to draw us to a place where we desire to commune with Him. At the point when we decide we want to feed our spirit man and accept Christ and are made new, we start a maturing process and gain a greater knowledge in communing with God. We start to gain wisdom, knowledge, and understanding of the things of Him. Before we come to Christ, we can read the Word of God and have no understanding of it or what it is trying to say to us. But once that spirit man comes alive, we start to gain understanding of Him and His Word.

If God gave us His Word to understand before we were capable of treasuring it, it would be like a friend giving another friend their most valued possession in the world only to know that they would throw it away and give it no value. God only gives His most valued possession to those who believe in it, desire it, and will honor it. Once we receive the gift God has for us and make that conscious decision to accept it, then our spirit man is made alive. It is at that point the Spirit of God is able to move in us. As we live our lives, there will always be that war inside of us, and the battle will always be between the three friends. The stronger the spirit man friend becomes, the less the other friends will intervene in the plans and future that God has for us. We need to learn to walk and feed the friend that can make us most alive and victorious. Let's embrace the most valued possession God has given to us, the Spirit of God who leads, guides, and gives life.

BURIED TREASURE

In whom are hidden all the treasures of wisdom and knowledge.

Colossians 2:3, NIV

Every year at Christmas, our family plays a gift exchange game. Family and friends gather together with various gifts placed in the middle of the room. Some gifts are small, some large, some wrapped beautifully, and some with very plain and simple wrapping. Everyone eagerly anticipates which gift they will receive. The challenge begins with which gift to pick, because the wrapping is not always an accurate representation of the gift that is inside. Some gifts that are chosen might be more desirable to one person than another. If one gets a gift they aren't very fond of, they can wait to trade, in hopes of obtaining a more desirable gift.

This reminds me of the day I encountered Leah at our women's Bible study. If she had been a gift that was presented and then unwrapped, she would not have necessarily been my choice for a gift, because her demeanor was harsh and abrasive. She was the type of person you might not desire to encounter again and definitely not one that you would choose for a friend. Sometimes when we encounter people, we are unaware of the treasure that lies within them. They present themselves with façades or wrappings to hide the hurt and pain inside. The gift exchange game presents the challenge of finding the most desirable gift. The wrapping is often deceptive and sometimes the gifts that appear to have the least value because of the wrapping end up being the greatest gifts. After observing Leah for a while, I wondered if beyond the hardened exterior there could be a treasure inside. I thought to myself time would certainly tell.

At our next encounter, her brokenness was revealed beneath a harsh covering. Solitude and isolation were a way of life and dying alone was definitely what she desired. The fear of spending an eternity in a pit as in her dream was the only thing that gripped her emotions. It allowed me a glimpse of what lay beneath the harsh wrapping. I wondered what was hidden in her heart. What façade was she wrapped in and what was really within? The wrapping that covered her heart was difficult to penetrate because she had learned early in life to trust no one. The course language and harsh responses were simply a defense mechanism to protect her from more hurt. If I had responded to her in a harsh manner or pulled away, then what was in her would have never been revealed. The process of time would unveil her heart and everything that lay beneath the hardness would be exposed. I knew that if she allowed me access, the love of Christ in me would reveal a tender heart concealed by many years of hurt and pain.

In Genesis we read about Eve and her rebellion against God. Her rebellion not only affected her life, but the trickle-down effect of sin is seen by all of us today. We all walk in sin and deal daily with sin because of one person's rebellion against God. The bondage of sin and the chains of rebellion were passed on to all generations from Eve. Some of the generations were the Israelites who spent years as slaves to the Egyptians and ended up wandering in the desert searching for their promised land for forty-years. If they had been obedient and not walked in the bondage of their ancestors, they would have reached their promised land in about eleven days. Just as the Israelites, we all have our Egypt.

I knew by looking at Leah that her past and present were at war inside her mind. The past had brought her to a place of destruction and death in every area of her life, and sin and rebellion had taken its toll. Her past brought her to a place of death spiritually and physically. So by a miracle that orchestrated her joining the Bible study and the relationship I was building with her, she found hope in her hopelessness and a peace she had never felt before. However, the fight and the turmoil continued inside, but her despair kept bringing her back to the study that God had orchestrated for her life.

Through this ongoing process I never realized the extent of her tremendous bondage. The sensation of the physical chains I saw binding her were unreal. The night I invited her to pray for salvation she expressed a concern that if her salvation experience wasn't significant and brought notable freedom and deliverance to her, then it wouldn't be enough. She was willing to die and face hell if freedom and deliverance from those physical chains weren't available. After listening to that comment, I wanted to scream out, "God is always enough!"

Instead, knowing my God was always faithful, I took her by the hand and prayed with her; how sweet that moment was for both of us. She wept and finally trusted me to embrace her. Right before my very eyes, when I took her to the cross, her healing started. God took her heart in His hands and immediately began to break those chains of bondage and began to heal her past hurts. It was a healing I knew only He could do.

If you know someone who is in bondage from past hurts and pain caused by the world, know there is a God able to love them beyond their hurt. Press in and guide them to a life of pure love and freedom through Christ. The only way to this freedom is through the cross—the cross where Christ bore all of our hurts and pain. Tell them He did it because He loved them that much. He would have done it even if they were the last person on earth. His love and compassion extends beyond all bondage and sin. Sometimes we need to forget about our lives and intercede on behalf of someone else's life. After all, our calling is to save souls, heal the sick, and bring hope to the hopeless.

WEB OF DECEIT

I have placed before you life and death, choose life!

Deuteronomy 30:19, MSG

In life there are two roads from which to choose. One road leads to eternal life, and one road leads to eternal death. If the choice is not apparent or obvious, then the answer to the question is given. Choose life!

The road leading to life is always placed before us. There is a miracle that will happen within us that may not be physically evident immediately, but we know that at the moment we believe and confess Christ the Spirit of God takes residence within our spirit making us new creatures in Christ Jesus. At the moment of our new birth experience, our inner man called the spirit man is changed, but everything external about us stays the same. Nothing changes externally or physically; we have the same looks, same weight and same hair color. Likewise, nothing automatically changes within our minds because we continue to have the same good or bad attitudes. If we were drama queens before, we will be drama queens after. It would be nice if God had made everything supernaturally change without any effort on our part. But if that were the case, we would not have a free will.

When we become new creatures in Christ we are given the manual that lists the promises of God that are available to us. That manual, which is the Bible, reveals the path and lays out all the directions and instructions for us to follow. Eternal life requires no work. The only requirement is to believe and confess, and then we have His gift. If it required works, it would be unobtainable. No man was able to live exactly by the letter of the law, which is why God had to offer His Son, Jesus Christ. We have eternal life or salvation because of God's mercy and grace. Mercy prevents us from receiving what we really deserve and grace allows us to obtain something that we do not deserve and are incapable of obtaining within ourselves.

The path of life that leads to death and destruction is different for everyone. For some, the need for a Savior doesn't seem necessary when every need they have is met. Others show the evidence of death and destruction because of the choices they made by participating in sin. Regardless, those who live like this should be desperate to understand their need for a Savior or Deliverer. In either case, death is imminent, and whether our life appears to be good or bad we will all stand before God one day. Those who have the Spirit of God living in them will spend eternity in heaven, and those who have rejected life with Christ will spend eternity separated from their Creator.

Walking the path in pursuit of the promises of God can be like walking a path of victory. Those of us whose lives were evidenced by sin and destruction were on a path where we were victims. But when we become new creatures in Christ we become the victor. Every choice in life that is made contrary to the Word of God causes us to be a victim, but every choice in life based on the Word of God causes us to become a victor. Let's consider the promises of God for a moment.

There is light, and there is darkness. If we live in sin, we are walking in darkness. If we know God and have a relationship with Him, then we walk in light. God is light, and in Him is no darkness. Darkness has no right to stay in the presence of light. Light will always overtake darkness, but for it to do so the light must be turned on. Before we come to know who God is, we are riddled with many things from our past: hurt, pain, insecurity, abuse, self-righteousness, pride, jealousy, lies and unforgiveness. The list of the things we possess in us is never-ending, and we have concealed many of these things in our heart. Some of us may never realize it, but we hide them in the dark recesses of our heart. When we hide things, we take ownership of them. When we know God, we have the assurance that He is a light unto our path. We have the choice to either allow those hidden dark things to be exposed, allowing the light to illuminate them, or to keep those hidden things in darkness. It's our heart, and it's our choice. Some of these hidden dark things we might have forgotten about because they were too humiliating or too hurtful. Some of them may have become just a part of who we are because they get us desired attention, making us feel loved. Some may bring us benefits in life, and the mind has reasoned that it is not really worth giving up those benefits, so we keep them hidden in the dark recesses of our hearts.

For example, picture a young woman who was abused as a child. The memories of the incidences are pushed back into the recesses of her mind. The desire to live is a fight, and depression is always knocking at her door. As she gets older she reaches out to men who don't respect her and who abuse her verbally and physically. She blames herself and feels unworthy of pure love. The cause of what took her onto the path of death and destruction is hidden in the recesses of her heart. She tries to forget, but because it is hidden in her heart it is still breeding destruction. Everything that is hidden in our heart has a root or a cause. Because we want to get through life we typically mask the symptoms of destruction instead of deal-ing with the root cause of them. It's like when we take medication for a headache, which may have been caused by a lack of fluids or even stress. Instead of adjusting our water intake or dealing with the stress that caused the headache we take medication to numb the symptoms.

Those who are new in Christ sometimes find the road to possessing the promises of God to be a journey of allowing hidden things in the heart to be exposed. If we do not expose our issues and problems it can lead to death and destruction. For example, in order for a spider to kill its prey, it has to weave a web to entangle it. The larger the web is, the greater the chance for the spider to catch and kill its prey. If the spider web is somehow destroyed, the surroundings will appear clean and tidy. However, if the spider is not destroyed it will eventually rebuild its web over and over again. The process of web reconstruction will continue until the builder of the web of destruction and death is destroyed. Many of us have spent our lives occasionally destroying those webs, but never killing the spider. If we never expose the cause of our issues eventually they will lead us to death and destruction. The only way to expose those hidden webs is by God's light, because if we live in Him there is no darkness. If we have webs in our life, they will attract nothing but darkness, and those spiders or issues need the light of God to be exposed.

Leah has come to know Christ but even with the promise of eternal life, she still deals with anger issues, bitterness, and unforgiveness in her heart. The webs of a life of sin and rebellion are still very evident, but what keeps her from returning to that life of sin and hiding issues in her heart are the promises that she holds in her. Every battle she fights—every web of destruction—was to keep her from the promise of hope.

However, she is now a believer and possesses the promise of eternal life with Christ. The battle now is to obtain the promises of God. The old man, the victim, must be transformed into a victor. Leah attempted in vain to mask her inner pain with alcohol, drugs, and rebellion. She got to a point where she could no longer trust men because too many had abused and defiled her. She knew what pleased them and knew what their wicked hearts would do for pleasure. Life became a pursuit for self-gain, even at the expense of others.

The only apparent promise was to put a wall of protection around the heart to conceal the webs, and never reveal the root. Could the victim be transformed into a victor? I realized Leah would have to face every perpetrator in her life, including her self-will and rebellion and then decide if she wanted to keep them in the recesses of her heart to build their web of death and destruction. Would she get to the place where she would allow the light of God to illuminate the darkness inside her heart so the webs of entanglement could be destroyed? Years of hardness were showing physically, and death was evident and quickly overtaking her.

The beginning of her life was unfair, and the game of life appeared to hold a losing hand. The saving grace is that the game isn't over until the last cards are dealt. The outcome was shifting, and the victim would now become a victor. If we play the right game, the rules are set to ensure our victory. Could she follow the rules? I know that with her history of rebellion, it was unlikely that she would.

One of the webs of entanglements in Leah's life was the abuse she suffered as a child. Death loomed over Leah, but the original cause of that pain in Leah's heart was unforgiveness. Who the actual perpetrator was is not relevant, the real issue was what was hiding in the recesses of her heart and that was unforgiveness. She questioned me as to why she should have to forgive the one who caused her so much hurt and pain. I told her the Bible says if you forgive men of their sin, your heavenly Father will also forgive you. It's a thought that was contrary to her natural, worldly thinking.

It's like when the salmon swim upstream while other fish are floating easily downstream. Salmon go against every law of nature by swimming upstream. They do so because they are on a mission, a mission to give birth. Salmon swim upstream for a purpose, and Leah eventually realized she had a mission. She has to make it upstream so she can give birth to her destiny and purpose, however contrary it may be to how she used to live. That same grace that forgives us also empowers us. It empowers us to forgive those who have wronged us. When we become a child of the King, we have the honor and privilege by grace to approach His throne and ask for His help in any situation or circumstance. When we ask the Spirit of God to empower us, He will give us strength. In this particular situation, the strength to forgive seemed impossible, but grace came through.

The web was exposed, and the predator of death was doomed for destruction. When it was exposed, tears of cleansing and healing flowed as unforgiveness left her heart. The web of entanglement and the predator were destroyed. Destruction and death due to unforgiveness immediately lost their grip and the control they had over her life. Now the tarnish of unforgiveness is being removed, and God's image is starting to reflect brightly in her. She now speaks of her abuser without bitterness and resentment. Tears of pain and hurt no longer flow and her heart is healing. She realizes what the web of unforgiveness is and hopefully will never be entangled in it again. The opportunity for us to become offended is never-ending, but there is greater empowerment living within us to eliminate webs. If you are a child of God and in need of empowerment, access to the throne room is never denied.

When the webs of evil inside the heart are exposed and the cause of destruction is exposed, death becomes less evident. Now, the *zoe* life—God kind of life—is beginning to illuminate from her, and the promises of God we all pursue are becoming evident in her.

As a young woman, she made foolish decisions that caused her great pain. Shame and guilt followed her, haunted and tormented her. Could she forgive herself? The Bible tells us that if we confess our sins, He is faithful and just to forgive us our sins and to cleanse us of all unrighteousness. Now every time she returns to the throne room she is able to access God's mercy and through His grace He empowers her to expose the webs of shame and guilt. It is the perpetrator of self-destruction that needs to be destroyed, but without the grace of God none of us are capable of forgiving ourselves, or others.

Some of the webs of deceit were brought on by others and some of the webs of deceit were initiated by self—all of them are in need of exposure to light. It is necessary to expose the cause and bring death to these webs. When we live as a victim, we are always on the defensive, always having to have a plan of self-protection. Self-preservation builds around the heart, never allowing the webs of deception to be exposed.

If we fail to walk in God's truth and fail to heed His warning, then the web of lies appears and rears its ugly head. Have you ever killed a cockroach in your home? If so, what is the thought that comes to your mind once the perpetrator is destroyed? There must be more! Similarly, that is how lies are bred. There is typically not just one. A lie is either exposed or it takes another lie to cover it. Some little creatures that are lies can breed and multiply very quickly; they can also become webs in our lives. Since God is a God of truth it is impossible for Him to lie. The lie breeds in the heart of man, and the web of deception grows. Lying is based on self-deception, and the perpetrator is fear and pride, among many other things. Cockroaches love damp, dark places, and that is where they love to breed. Unless lies are exposed to the light they will continue to breed. When a cockroach roams into the open light, we take the opportunity to kill it. The best way to kill a lie is to expose it. The good news is that God will help us destroy those webs of lies.

We read earlier that God is light, and in Him there is no darkness. He is also a God of truth. He always operates within the boundaries of His Word. He is a God of justice and cannot step out of what His Word says. He has placed the road of life before us and has given us the option to choose that road. So here are the two roads: one that leads to life and one to death. If we choose the road to death, God will not stop us. He has given us free will to do as we choose. If we take the road to life, it will lead us to His blessings. If we choose the road to death, we forfeit those blessings, and we will reap those curses in our lives.

A father can warn a child about the dangers of fire, but if she is not guarded and protected, she is in danger of being hurt by the flames. As children grow, they are trusted to heed parental warnings of danger. If the child chooses to step outside of those boundaries, it is because of her free will. If the child chooses to not heed caution, she will suffer the consequences of the fire. As children of God, we are given cautions and warnings. If we heed, the light will continue to illuminate the road that leads to the promises of God. But if we don't heed the caution, then the warning light grows dim and the blessings of God are not illuminated in our lives; we end up getting burned by those fires.

I explained to Leah the heart is deceitful above all things and desperately wicked. When the heart is exposed and illuminated by God, the light will illuminate the darkness. God knows our hearts and knows every detail of every web and the root cause of every single perpetrator before we ever expose them. For us to think we have no webs in the recesses of our hearts is truly deception. God knows our hearts, but to conquer the webs we must allow Him access. We must allow His light to illuminate every web and deception in our hearts. If we ask, He will never leave us unkempt, dirty, or messy. When we allow Him access, He will be there to help us clean out the recesses of our hearts no matter how ugly and dirty. Oh, if you only knew how great His mercy is, how great His grace is, and how great His love is! After conquering the webs of deceit we are able to place our focus on our true pursuit in life and that is one for clean hands and a pure heart.

SHACKLED

I'm cutting you free from the ropes of your bondage.

Nahum 1:12, MSG

Our existence on earth is as a blinking of an eye; our lifetime is but a moment. When we compare our lifetime to eternity, our life is a very short segment of time. Eternity is not anything we can see with our physical eye or touch with our natural senses, but nevertheless eternity exists. Every decision we make during this walk of life impacts not only our future walk on earth, but also affects our eternity. The failure to make right decisions regarding our eternity is often based on the fact that we fail to see what the future holds. Sometimes our future may appear hopeless to us because we fail to realize the impact our decisions have on those around us. We don't realize that our decisions and the way we live impact the people we encounter on a daily basis. What we are born into may not necessarily be what we end up doing in life. We are created with a free will. Our lives are predestined, our path prepared, spiritual gifts given, and futures planned before we were created. Because we have free will, God allows us to make our own decisions regarding the path we choose to walk. Our destiny, even though it's already been established, is driven by our decisions.

Let's take a look at the life of a man who was chosen before birth to be a great influence to his people and see how his life plays out because of wrong decisions and disobedience.

The book of Judges relates the story of Samson who was born to a woman said to be barren. God told her that Samson would deliver His people out of the hand of the enemy and would have supernatural strength. Specific instruction was given to her that a razor should never touch his head. He was to be a Nazarite from birth, never to eat anything defiled, drink strong drink, or cut his hair. He was born with a vow of purity to remain undefiled before the Lord. As he grew, the Spirit of the Lord came upon him and gave him supernatural strength. His strength was so great that he tore a lion apart with his bare hands. He was a real man who possessed supernatural power and strength.

But, Samson had a downfall: a desire for women. His God-ordained purpose was to live the great life of a Nazarite and remain pure in his thoughts and everything he did. But even though Samson was called to be a Nazarite, he still had the free will to choose God's purpose and plan, or his own desires, just as we do. Samson knew that the Philistine women were enemies to the Jewish people, and for Samson to fulfill his purpose with God, he was to stay away from them.

When we go through life, obstacles come at us and the way we choose to deal with them decides our future. One day, Samson feasted his eyes on a Philistine woman named Delilah. Samson's Philistine enemies strove to know the secret of Samson's power and from where his great strength came, because they wanted to kill him. Delilah's job was to entice him and find out what his secret was so the Philistines could overpower him. She started out by simply asking, "Please tell me where you get your strength. What is it that would cause you to lose your strength?" We need to listen carefully to the statement that Delilah made to Samson regarding his strength. Satan is a deceiver and is always there to eavesdrop to find out where our weaknesses are so he can set a trap of destruction.

Would you see a red flag if someone persistently sought the secret to the source of your strength?

The things of this world always entice and look desirable to us. Samson should have never desired Delilah in the first place. His eyes looked at her, and the longer he looked, the more he longed and desired her. How many times have we looked and longed for things to later find out we should not have touched? The enemy sets the trap of deception and neglects to tell us the consequences of yielding to the desires of our flesh.

Delilah was beautiful and pleasing to the eyes and his flesh. Perhaps initially, the statement that Delilah asked him sounded cute and sexy, "Please tell me how I can capture you." Bondage never cries out and says, "Capture me, and I will destroy you." Bondage always entices with empty promises of superficial pleasure. The superficial pleasure tantalizes the flesh as the chains of bondage continue to wrap around and around until there is no hope of freedom and no hope of the chains being broken. The heart continues to search for answers, but none are found. The pain of the bondage heightens and the heart cries out for something to ease the pain; the vicious cycle of sin begins in our lives.

The story continues and Samson becomes a bit cocky and forgets why he has his supernatural powers. He starts toying with her and tells her that if he is bound with seven fresh bowstrings, then he would become weak and be like any other man. So Delilah did as Samson said. She bound him up with the bowstrings and Samson's enemies waited to kill him. Samson was joking with her and he jumped up and broke off the bowstrings.

Just as the Philistines waited to kill Samson, Satan lurks and lies in wait for the opportune time to wrap us up in another chain of bondage. Those chains can be alcohol, drugs, or illicit sex, and can cause our hearts to become numb from the pain of these vices. Our hearts are pleasured without ever realizing the chains of bondage are gripping us tighter and tighter.

Delilah, realizing that she was going to have to get more creative, started playing the victim. She says to Samson, "Look, you have mocked me and told me lies. Now, please tell me what will catch you and what gives you your strength." Samson plays with her emotions again and says, "If you tie me with new ropes, I will become weak." So she bound him while the Philistines waited, but he breaks them again.

At this point Delilah is getting frustrated with him. She becomes more dramatic and manipulative and tells him that he has mocked her and told her enough lies. She goes for his heart and tells him, "How can you say, 'I love you,' when your heart doesn't love me and you lied to me? You have mocked me and told me lies three times, and you still haven't told me where you get your great strength."

Just like Delilah's deception of Samson, the world plays a game of deception with our hearts, and we never realize it. God created us with a tender heart that is full of compassion, and longs for intimacy and pure love. Sometimes our heart longs for love, and we end up selling out for a cheap counterfeit to satisfy our longing. It is the deception and desires of self that squelch the compassion and keeps us from finding that place of intimacy and pure love in Christ.

Instead of Samson leaving to a place of safety he stayed to listen and play with his enemy. The Bible tells us that Delilah pestered him continually with her words and pressed him so much that his soul was vexed to death and he told her all that was in his heart. Samson said to her, "No razor shall ever come upon my head, for I have been a Nazarite to God from my mother's womb, and if I am shaven, then my strength will leave me, and I will become weak, and be like any other man."

Like Samson, our first mistake can be to look long and desire hard. Our second mistake is made when we listen to lies that promise a better way contrary to God's perfect plan. Samson was pestered continually by Delilah's words. He listened and listened until he was so tired of listening that his mind, will, and emotions were brought to a state of confusion and destruction; he told her everything in his heart.

We can become so pestered day in and day out that our mind, will, and emotions are brought to a state of confusion and destruction. We end up disclosing all the secrets of our hearts. Sometimes it feels like we pour out our life and tell everything that we have hidden in our heart that is sacred to us. We sell out the treasure within and feel like there is no hope of retrieving what has been stolen. We sell out our heart; worse yet, we give it away for free. The perpetrator that comes to destroy and steal the things in our heart doesn't value our purpose or where we spend eternity and that betrays the very depth of our being.

Delilah realized that he had told her all his heart and sent for the enemy who was trying to kill Samson. She lulled him to sleep on her lap and called for a man to shave the seven locks of his head; then began his torment as his strength left him.

He gave into the voice, and the deception overtook him. Now both the strength that enabled him to resist the enemy and the voice that vexed him were gone. The person who desired the pleasures of the world was not able to enjoy them any longer because they brought on destruction. The very thing that appeared pleasing to the eyes and whispered tantalizing promises for Samson allowed the enemy to destroy him.

Samson woke up and thought he would be able to go out and shake himself free. He did not realize all his supernatural powers were gone. The enemy that Samson had conquered in the past now overpowered him. They put out his eyes, bound him, and placed him in prison. He was now unable to overcome the powers of the enemy because he had bowed to the desires of his flesh. While Samson was bound, his eyes could no longer deceive him. What had God promised him? Could he ever be set free from the chains that bound him?

During the time he was in the Philistine prison, the hair on his head began to grow back. The enemy was joyous that they had conquered the Nazarite and gathered to offer sacrifices to their god. They desired entertainment and called for Samson from prison so he could perform for them. Samson was stationed between the pillars that supported the temple. Then Samson prayed to the Lord, saying, "Lord God, remember me, I pray! Strengthen me and give me power just once more. God, all I want to do is with one blow take vengeance on my enemy for taking my two eyes!" Samson took hold of the pillars that supported the temple. Bracing against them, he pushed with all his might and the temple fell on all the people who were in it. While the temple walls were falling, Samson said, "Let me die with the enemy." So all the people he killed at his death were more than he had killed during his lifetime.

When we get to the place where we have released all the secrets of our heart and they are made a mockery by the enemy, know God is there waiting to offer a safe place in which to dwell. Some of us have faced death's door because the desires of the flesh have led us to that place of destruction, but God in His infinite mercy has guarded and protected our lives.

As we journey through life, many of us do not realize the bondage we carry or have created due to situations and choices we have made in our lives both past and present. They are chains that bind us as we make our way through relationships with husbands, children, friends, and coworkers. We do not realize the way we have lived in the past reflects on our future.

Satan waits for the most appropriate time to sneak in to capture the secrets of our hearts. What we need to understand in Samson's story is that he chose to fulfill his dreams and desires while lost and in a weakened state. He sought forgiveness from the one person who strengthened him from the beginning. When we turn from God's purpose and plan, His mercy is always there to bring restoration to our lives. When we are at our weakest, He is still there to strengthen us to fight the enemy that has set out to destroy us.

Once we defeat the enemy, we are able to fulfill our purpose and plan. What took Samson to his death were his eyes. I believe when Samson lost his sight, he lost the ability to see those worldly desires and was able to see his true plan and purpose again. Sometimes it takes us losing something to realize what has been deceiving us. Not being able to see the distractions of life allows us the opportunity to focus on the One who created us and to see the original plan and purpose for which we were created. Sometimes we believe God will never forgive us when we have walked in sin and have the cloud of guilt and shame hanging over us. But in His infinite mercy, He is able to forgive and endue us with power all over again.

CAPTIVITY

I no longer call you slaves, because a master doesn't con-
fide in his slaves. Now you are my friends, since I have
told you everything the Father told me.

John 15:15, NLT

Imagine having everything you need and everything your heart
ever desired. Is there one of you who would be willing to walk away
from it all? Is there someone you love for whom you would lay it all
down? If we think of an enemy, a person who has betrayed, cursed
or stolen from you, would you sacrifice yourself to save him or her?
Some would say they could give it up, possibly, for people they love
or are dear to their hearts. Could you give it up for your enemies?

There was a King who owned all and lacked nothing. He
reigned over the most glorious kingdom we could ever imagine. He
left His kingdom of riches, glory and honor for the most despised
man we could imagine, so the despised could experience life. He
paid the price and the penalty of sin owed by the despised man. The
King asked nothing in return, but hoped that he would tell others
of the King who left His kingdom for that man. The King who left
His kingdom and everything in it desires that we allow Him to be
King and Lord of our lives so we can inherit the riches of His kingdom. He left a place of security, riches, honor, and the glory of His
kingdom for you so that you can experience the good life and all of

the promises of God. Would you be willing to accept the sacrifice of the King, and are you willing to share it with others?

I remember the day I heard about that King who left His kingdom for me. He had left His place of eternal glory so I could have eternal life. The God I was serving at the time was not attainable because of the confines of the religion I was raised in. God was very distant to me. I knew human love, but I did not know the love of a heavenly Father. I accepted the call to know the Father without hesitation because I was in need of hope and a promise for my future. Finally, the love of the King who laid down everything for me was now the owner of my heart. My heart was still held in captivity by the bondage it had once known. My heart could not grasp that He could love me so much that He would lay down His life for me. People would look me in the eyes and declare that God loved me, but the guilt and shame of my undeserving past would prevent me from looking directly back at them. My heart, which was set free from the prison of religion, did not know how to truly be free. It's not that I didn't long for freedom, but the reality was, how could I walk free from captivity when my heart had never known freedom?

My past spoke of unworthiness and unforgiveness and my heart questioned the new-found freedom. I remember standing in church and the people singing the song, "Friend of God." My eyes would scan the people who declared with such freedom and liberty that they were friends of God. My heart questioned how they could be so bold to declare God could be their friend. How could that be possible? My unworthiness kept me from declaring these words. The shame and the guilt of my past and the bondage that held my heart in captivity battled with the truth that declared God loved me. Truth will always prevail over lies, light always prevails over darkness, and greatest of all, love prevails over guilt and shame. Over time the truth of God's love broke the captivity in my heart and His love encapsulated it, opening the prison doors. Then my mouth declared from the depths of my heart, "I am a friend of

God." I realized at that moment the One who left His glorious kingdom left it for me, and I was finally able to open my mouth to declare His love for others to know.

Love covers a multitude of sin—that is the saying right? It wasn't the voices of guilt and shame of the past that covered my sin. It wasn't a voice bringing constant reminders of previous failures or inadequacies that covered my sin. It wasn't paying a debt owed or suffering appropriate consequences for past errors. It was love, His love. It was a love that prompted the King to leave His kingdom. It was the love that caused the King to leave all His riches and all His glory for me to be set free from the debt I owed of every wrong decision, every sin, and every shortcoming in my life.

Leah was so mercifully delivered from the kingdom of darkness and now walks in the kingdom of light because of the King who left His kingdom. The transfer from the kingdom of darkness into the kingdom of light took her from a place of hopelessness to the promise of eternal life with hopes of deliverance—a deliverance that would conquer death, bondage, and destruction. Prison doors had been opened, and the captive had been set free. Could the captive now walk in freedom, and could the promise of freedom really be hers?

The Israelites were held in bondage for 430 years by the Egyptians. They were slaves who were given a promise of hope, promise of a better life, promises of the prison doors being opened, and promises of freedom. Twelve Israelite spies went into the land promised to them. It was a land of abundance where slavery would not rule. They saw the greatness of the land that had been promised to them with their own eyes. They touched the promises and tasted the promise. Upon returning, only two of the twelve reported victory and the other ten reported defeat. The prison doors of captivity were opened for all twelve, but only two held on to that promise. The two who came back with a good report heard the voice of the One who declares love, and that superseded the voice that declared bondage. For the other ten spies the prison doors were also opened, but they chose not to leave the captivity of their prison because, although they heard the voice of the promise, they didn't believe it and would die in the wilderness.

The whole camp of Israelites listened to the negative reports of the ten. Physically they were delivered from Egypt, but Egypt was never delivered from their hearts. They were set free, but they didn't know freedom and couldn't understand it. The bondage from which they were being delivered eventually killed them because of their unbelief. The voice that declared the lies of the past overshadowed the voice of truth, hope, freedom, and love. They listened to the negative reports and the deception of captivity bound them.

Leah chose to enter into the Promised Land, the land of freedom; every debt of sin from her past was paid in full. The prison doors were opened and the promise was deliverance. The worldly effects were still evident in her life, but the debt had been paid. Could the captive walk free from captivity? The locks had been removed from the chains of bondage, but could the chains be removed? She had been forgiven, but could Leah forgive herself? Her sins had been forgotten, but could Leah forget them herself? Maybe she could forgive herself and allow the chains to be removed, but could others forgive her and could others forget? Would she hold herself in bondage and die with an undelivered promise of freedom or would others hold her in bondage and captive to her past?

Those chains that bind us are the chains of our past. The locks are things that we participated in and chose to do. We can accept Jesus Christ as the Lord and Savior of our life, but if we choose to continue to walk in our past, then we can never walk into the promises God has for us. The children of Israel were always looking to their past. They were slaves having to perform dirty rotten jobs for the pharaoh of Egypt. They hated every minute that they worked for the Egyptians; nothing they worked for or what they possessed was theirs. They didn't even own their own children. The minute that God set them free, they walked into their freedom, and rejoiced. But after a couple of days in the desert, after their release from the bondage of slavery, they began to look back. When they looked back, all they saw was what they thought was good. They actually thought that living and working in bondage was better than walking free in the desert. Instead of looking to their future— a future of hope, dreams, and promises from God—they chose to look back at their past, and they desired it.

Leah sought something better and knew that her life had been filled with wrong choices and pain. But she sometimes wondered if the life she had left was better than the one she had chosen to walk in. It is difficult to get people who have come from a torrid past to realize that what they had wasn't as wonderful as they remember it to be. Satan, the deceiver, makes sure that he masks the pain and hurts of the past and when he brings it to our memory, makes sure that he only shows us what we thought was good. He wants our eyes focused on our past so we cannot move forward. In order to move forward, we must keep our eyes on the road ahead. We need to remember that we were captives of our past and we need to become victors in our future. God is waiting to walk us into victory—into the Promised Land—that He has prepared for His people. Let's not be slaves to our past, our bondage, and those chains that held us captive; let's walk to our freedom never looking back!

OVERSHADOWED

In the Messiah, in Christ, God leads us from place to place in one perpetual victory parade. Through us, He brings knowledge of Christ. Everywhere we go, people breathe in the exquisite fragrance. Because of Christ, we give off a sweet scent rising to God, which is recognized by those on the way to salvation—as aroma redolent with life.

2 Corinthians 2:14–15 (MSG)

When Eve walked in the garden and communed with God, she abided in a place where evil was never present. In the middle of that garden was the knowledge of good and evil. God warned her that if she ate of the tree of the knowledge of good and evil, then she would die. Within the garden where they lived, everything was good just as God wanted it. When God spoke creation into existence, He said it was good. Eve never knew of evil until she desired something more than what God had provided. The voice of deception, Satan, in the form of a serpent, spoke lies to her and told her there was something greater out there for her. She looked, longed, listened and finally ate. Eve immediately experienced something she had never known before—evil. Adam and Eve then hid themselves because of fear and both discovered they were naked. Prior to Eve stepping outside of the boundaries God had set, she had never known what fear was. Fear had not existed in the garden and now it caused them to hide from God, the One who loved them. Without the knowledge of evil, Adam and Eve would not have known fear. Fear can add a variety of issues into our lives.

When we decide to go out into a storm, we protect ourselves with an umbrella. If we walk out from under the covering of an umbrella, we open ourselves up to the elements of nature to saturate us. In our spiritual lives we can live under the shadow of the Almighty. There He provides a safety and protection we can live under. We can live there until we decide to remove ourselves from that protected place.

For example, an infant who is nurtured and loved knows no fear and knows no evil. When evil is introduced into her life, the child will start to experience fear. The child may experience bad dreams or uneasiness by watching certain things on television or by hearing stories that can breed fear. We live in a world where we are surrounded by a real element of evil that will taint us. When my mind is battling with fear, I love to quote, "He who dwells in the secret place of the Most High shall abide under the shadow of the Almighty, He is my refuge and my fortress, in Him I shall trust." In saying this it helps me to remember where I abide or live. It takes me to that safe place of protection, free from fear. It is under the umbrella of the Almighty that I am protected from the elements of the world. How sweet and precious that place is. It is in that place I find a peace that passes all understanding. When the storms of life come they are much easier to handle in that place of peace and rest.

Before that whole sin and fear scenario existed with Adam and Eve, God knew man would mess it up. If we were put in Eve's place, most of us would have made the same decisions, much as we now make decisions that bring evil and fear into our lives and those around us. God knew Eve would mess up and He knows we will mess up, but God has it all figured out. He is constantly looking to find a heart loyal to Him. He isn't looking for someone perfect, but someone who desires to be loyal. If only we could just say, "I will choose to hide in the secret place of the Most High and live under the shadow of the Almighty." Then the Spirit of God hovers; His presence is always existent and is ever present. We are always surrounded by God's presence and we have been created to commune with Him. When we step into sin or live in sin, we are separating ourselves from His presence. At that point we lose the ability to walk and talk with Him, and we lose that ever-present presence of God inside of us.

The Bible tells a story of an angel who appeared to a woman named Mary. The angel told her not to be afraid because she had found favor with God and she would become the deliverer of the Messiah. I believe that was a call for her to live in the safe place, the secret place, and under His shadow. The request was made, and the plan and purpose was set in front of her. She responded to the angel, "How can this be?"

The angel answered, "The Holy Spirit will come upon you, and the power of the Most High will overshadow you: therefore, also, that Holy One who is to be born will be called the Son of God." Mary had a choice placed before her. Where would she decide to position herself? Would she choose to abide under the shadow of the Almighty allowing the Spirit of God to hover over her? Mary pondered and responded, "Let it be to me according to your word." Mary asked, "How can this be," since she didn't know a man, but she did not start making excuses. She didn't say, "I'm less than perfect; I lack the necessary qualification; I'm so unworthy; I think you need to find another; If you only knew my past; I was never chosen for anything in my life." She simply responded, "Let it be according to your word."

Mary knew in her heart that if she yielded and positioned herself under the shadow of the Almighty, under that umbrella of God, it would bring her favor. She knew the power of the Most High would overshadow her and take the void and emptiness inside her and bring life to it.

What does *overshadow* mean exactly? Overshadow means the impartation of power, hovering, or complete covering to include transformation. When Mary yielded to the overshadowing, she allowed the impartation of power by the Holy Spirit. She allowed the hovering, the complete covering of the power of the Most High to bring light to a dark place, and life where there was void. If we choose not to live in that shadow, we choose to walk in darkness. We create a void in our lives and we allow our hearts and lives to be opened up for the accuser, Satan, to come in and steal and destroy God's plan and purpose for our lives. Mary could have chosen not to live under that shelter, and if she would have done that, she would have missed out on the greatest purpose and plan on earth: Giving birth to the Messiah, the One who would save the world from itself.

Just as the angel told Mary not to fear for she had found favor with God, everyone who chooses to live in the secret place of the Most High and live under that shadow and doesn't fear, has also found favor. It is our choice to live in that place under the shadow of the Almighty where the Spirit of God can overshadow us. God wants to bring His life into our lives and light to the dark places that are in our hearts. In that place of overshadowing there is an impartation of power, and complete covering that can bring transformation to our lives. In that place, if we allow the Spirit of God to move, we can receive our promise and the will of God that will bring life into us and into every life that we reach out to touch.

God's desire is that we achieve what seems impossible to us. God will take the natural, the sinner, and will turn it into the supernatural just as He did with Mary. Remember, He looks to find those hearts that are loyal to Him. That is the key. God desires to have total access to our hearts and lives. We have to give God the key and allow Him in because God will not open the door unless we give Him access. God will never take any authority and access we don't give Him, and will never enter into a place He is not invited. Once we give Him access to our hearts and yield completely, we set ourselves in alignment with His plan and the presence of the Spirit of God covers us. From that point on He can move in us and overshadow us, we are able to walk in the presence, power and authority, and can commune constantly with Him.

In the world we live in, most people are only pleased with us when we do something to earn their respect or approval. God is looking for the loyal at heart. When we allow God to overshadow us and allow Him access to work in our hearts and do His will, He is well pleased. Nothing we could do would ever be good enough to attain that covering and overshadowing that He desires to have in our lives. Mary was blessed among women because she yielded to the plan and purpose of God. She yielded to the overshadowing of the Most High God and became highly favored. God is looking for those today whom He can overshadow and upon whom He can cast His favor. A favor that will be noticed in a dark world and be a light to the hopeless and a life of power to reach those who are lost.

There are two roads that are placed before us: the good road, which is the overshadowing; and the evil road, which positions us outside of the covering and outside of the shielding. God tells us to step in and come under His covering. He says, "I will shield you, and I will protect you." When we set ourselves in alignment with the Spirit of God, our lives will be changed and transformed, and the Spirit of God can move in us and over us, and it will be life-changing and permanent.

When we walk under that covering, we can change the lives of the hurting and hopeless. Mary didn't have to think about her response when the angel of the Lord overshadowed her and told her she was going to give birth to the Messiah; her response was instant. We need to become like Mary, humble and acceptable, a pure vessel before God and find that place of overshadowing so we can receive empowerment and have the ability to change things around us.

The key is our hearts must become vulnerable and come to a place of complete brokenness, allowing Him to embrace us, our hurts, and to heal our hearts completely. In that place of brokenness, we allow God to move in our lives and He will plant a vision in us. Our future is then laid out before us, and we can walk in the power of the Most High. We are given the assurance that we can walk in His will, His ways, and for His glory. Our destiny will be revealed, and we can walk in wholeness, with clean hands and pure hearts.

To be overshadowed by the power of God is a process of transformation. Our lives can be changed by the weighty power of God. When we place ourselves under God's umbrella and are overshadowed, we hear His voice, His power is imparted, the will of God made clear, and the presence of the Holy Spirit is revealed.

If we choose not to abide under that shadow and we take the evil road, then we lead oppressed lives and live in a world that is controlled by the enemy, opening ourselves up for demons to hover and press us down. Their job is to take us to their evilest end, an end of eternal darkness and death. Satan doesn't want us to succeed and walk in the path and the ways that God has chosen for us. He wants to rob us of our eternity and our destiny in God. The shame and oppression we experience in our lives is from the enemy, and if we give in to the enemy's plan, he will stay because we've allowed him to stay. If we continue to live in the shame and oppression the enemy has put on us through our life experiences, then he has a claim, a stronghold, on our lives. But when we decide to turn every hurt and pain over to God, the enemy has no platform and will not stay.

When we decide to hide nothing and open our hearts to show God everything then the enemy has no authority. At that point we are free to see the hope in our future and walk in that ever-present presence of Christ and walk in the sweet smelling aroma of the shadow of the Almighty.

Our lives need to get to a place where we can allow God to accept our vulnerability so He can take us to a place of complete brokenness. We need to allow Him to embrace our weaknesses and turn them into strengths. It's like taking a flower and crushing it to be able to release its aroma. The fragrance of vulnerability is a sweet smelling perfume to our Savior. He delights in the sweet aroma of our openness. At the point of openness, the Spirit of God will come and commune with our spirit man and will release a fresh anointing of His Spirit on us. When we possess that open spirit, our hearts will be opened to Him and the things that are not of Him will be erased. That gives us access to purity of heart and clean hands to come close to Him.

Being able to accomplish total openness can be difficult for a person who has lived a worldly life and has learned not to trust. To bring ourselves to openness can reveal hurt and pain from our past, things we have chosen to hide and keep secret. Those secrets are sins that we still harbor and evidence of Satan's little hold he still has on our life. If we harbor hurt and pain, it is a type of oppression, and it hinders our communion with God if we live and stay in that place. Our goal is to open those dark closets to a loving Father who is willing and able to offer healing, deliverance and hope. In that hope we can walk into His shelter, overshadowing, and protection from Satan's attack. Life will not always be easy. Troubles and trials will still come, and Satan will still be there to try and dangle our past in front of our face, but in God's eyes we are seen as perfect and without blemish.

In that purity we can approach God's throne and be completely saturated in His presence. His love breaks down every barrier and turns a hardened heart into one that desires to commune with Him. My challenge to you: If you have never opened your heart and given Him the keys, do it today. Ask Him to take those hurts and pain and cover you with His sweet presence. At the moment you ask, feel His love cover you and you will know that you are being overshadowed. Let's transform our lives into a sweet smelling aroma for our Savior.

GIANT KILLER

Could it be any clearer? Our old way of life was nailed to
the cross with Christ, a decisive end to that sin-miserable
life—no longer at sin's every beck and call!

Romans 6:6 (MSG)

After spending more time with Leah I began to see the value of
what was inside of her. I had spent many years in church never
realizing that I had a judgmental heart. It was a difficult process
for me to truly understand that we are not to judge anyone regardless of their past. Even though she and I had lived two different
lives, I knew Leah had something to teach me, and others as lost
as she had been. At this time, I was to set aside my judgmental
heart because God spoke to me to mentor and help mold her into
a mighty woman of God.

I thought of a fashion designer who sits and designs a dress.
The designer has an image in her mind of how this special garment will look. She searches and spends time choosing the right
fabric for the dress she intends to create. In the end, it is the seam-
stress who threads and pieces the fabric into a garment, bringing
the creative idea into reality. But it is still the designer's creation.
God brings people into our lives to fashion them into the image
that He originally wanted them to be. In getting to know Leah, I
understood she was a valuable piece whom God had created. He
had carefully chosen the fabric out of which he would create her.

Most people might view her life and past and reject her as a "used garment." But when God worked on my heart and began to tear down the walls of a judgmental attitude, He opened my eyes to see the valuable treasure that He had created.

This reminds me of the story of David. He was a sheepherder by trade and the youngest of eight brothers. God had a plan for David and David had a heart after God; everything David did was to please God. One day, God sent a prophet named Samuel to David's house to find the young man and anoint him to be king of Israel. Initially, David's father thought for sure one of his older sons would be king. But God doesn't choose us by our physical stature or what the world sees or values as greatness. He chooses us according to our hearts. God's desire is for us to have a loyal heart to serve Him. Samuel realized that none of David's brothers were what God had planned. As soon as David was presented to Samuel, he knew that God wanted him anointed as king. At that moment Samuel anointed David and God's plan and purpose for David's life was planted into his heart. After David was anointed, he soon realized there were many journeys that had to be completed before he actually reigned as king over Israel.

During this time Israel had many enemies; among them were the Philistines. The Philistines hated the Israelites and wanted to make them servants. They didn't believe in God or know how faithful God was to Israel. God chose David because He knew that David would fight by his faith in God. That was important because it would ensure David's victory over the Philistines. There had to be a purpose and David had to know the purpose was far greater than his understanding of the situation. There was a war to be fought and God chose David to conquer the enemy. David already knew this because it had been planted in his heart. David went before the reigning king of Israel, Saul, and said he would kill the Philistine giant. This giant was a warrior of many years and was huge! He stood nine feet tall and wore battle gear that weighed hundreds of pounds. David was just a young man of normal stature, but confident in what had been planted in his heart. He knew that if he didn't stand for the people of Israel and defeat the giant, the Israelites would become slaves. Everybody else was afraid of this giant because he was huge and because he taunted them continually. The Israelites grew weary because of the endless taunts and lies. David had enough. He was going to fight this giant and defeat him. He wasn't afraid because he knew that God was on his side. He knew that if he went out there and took that step of faith and stood in the face of this giant God would go with him and provide a way for him to kill and defeat this giant.

It was at this point David gained purpose in his pursuit. He was determined that others would know his God. As a shepherd, David had been delivered from a lion and a bear and had defeated and killed them with his bare hands because God was on his side. David knew that he was not created to serve the enemies of God, but that he was called to be a servant of the Most High God. David's fight was a physical one. He needed to choose his weapons of warfare to defeat this giant. And he decided on a slingshot and five smooth stones. David had used these many times before and utilized them to protect his flocks from harm. He was determined to kill this giant just as he had killed his other attackers. David stood before the giant with only a slingshot and five smooth stones in hand declaring his faith in God. Who did the giant think he was to make fun of God? The giant laughed in David's face and dared him to come closer. David did and took one shot at the giant burying a stone in the middle of his forehead. The giant fell to the ground. David went over to him, drew the giant's sword, and cut off his head. The rest of the Philistine army retreated, and that day David delivered the Israelites from slavery. David never saw the giant bigger than God's deliverance. David knew that his God was worth fighting for.

Just like David, we are created to serve the Most High God and not serve the enemies of the world. God created each of us with a plan and a purpose from the very beginning of our lives. Many of us have never realized that we are pieces to a big puzzle. As part of the puzzle we have a responsibility to bring others to the saving knowledge and grace of Jesus Christ. It's the same saving knowledge that many of us have come to know. We are created to walk the path that is set in front of us and deliver others from the giants in their lives. The giants that taunt us are there to break us down; to defeat the plan and purpose God created in each of us.

Our hearts can become hardened by listening day in and day out to the constant taunting of the enemy. When we constantly hear defeatist words being spoken to us and we focus on the problems in our life, then we can lose sight of the purpose that has been planted in us. We need to be like David and fight our giants while focusing on the victory and the vision ahead, instead of focusing on the giants that taunt us.

When David fought his battles, he had to fight them physically. He had to possess great physical strength to be able to conquer and inherit the things that God promised him. Today, I thank God our battles can be fought spiritually instead of physically. Although at times I think it might be easier to take a sword in our hand and conquer and kill the enemies who are out to destroy us. Unlike David, we are not able to see what we fight because our fights are in the spirit realm. Many times it is difficult to determine who our enemies really are. Are our enemies the day-to-day people and situations we encounter? No, we are fighting for a greater cause. That cause is the lost, and the fight is against a spiritual giant named Satan who has come to steal from us, kill us, and destroy anyone who hasn't come to the saving knowledge of Christ and the understanding that God is always faithful to deliver us from our enemies.

Every day, some fight battles with their spouse, children and co-workers. We fight to live and exist in this world, but our true battle ought to be for a lost and dying world. The kind of battle that brings life to people who are bound by giants and aren't even aware of it. The battles against our giants are fought spiritually because we have the Spirit of God living in us. He alone gives us the strength and power to fight these spiritual battles. There are many giants in this world desiring to take us captive and hold us in bondage. Their desire is to bring spiritual death to us. We choose whom we are going to be a servant to and what holds and grips us in bondage. If we don't remove these giants from our lives and destroy them as David did, then we will end up serving them and miss out on completing the puzzle God intends for us to complete.

When we become a follower of Christ we are able to commune with Him. He equips and empowers us to conquer those giants in our lives. When we defeat these giants, we are able to obtain the promises that God has for us. What is required of us? Ears to hear the plan, a heart to obey every direction, and a desire to possess at all cost. To some people, it may have appeared impossible and utterly ridiculous for David to conquer and kill the giant. But he knew his victory was imminent because of the faith he had in God and God is faithful at all times.

Our victory is imminent because we have the Spirit of God living in us. The most important lesson we must learn is that we need ears to hear the plan, a heart to obey every direction, and a desire to possess at all cost. When the Spirit of God lives in us we can boldly stand in the face of our giants and declare victory and possess it with full assurance.

SANCTIFICATION

To make her holy and clean, washed by the cleansing of
God's word.

Ephesians 5:26 (NLT)

In the previous chapter we spoke about David and the battle he
fought against the giant Goliath. The battle David fought was very
physical and many of us would have wimped out. Today the battles
we fight are not physical, but we have to choose our weapons of
warfare as David did. Our warfare has to be fought spiritually and
we need to be prepared for this kind of battle in order to stand in
the face of our giants. David did not choose the five smooth stones
randomly. He took his time to examine, looking for the smoothest,
most perfect stones that if enough force was applied, would penetrate the thick skull of his adversary and deliver death.

When we fight our battles spiritually, we must become strate-
gic weaponry like the smooth stones and be ready to be launched
at our adversaries at all times making sure to do deadly damage to
the enemy's camp. We develop skills to fight and become effective
soldiers by the Word of God, which washes us and sanctifies our
lives. If David had used a stone with rough edges, it probably would
not have been the most effective weapon and the enemy would
surely have defeated David. If we allow our weaponry to become
dull and unused by not allowing the Word of God to wash us, then
we are like a stone that sits in a stagnant place where the water can-

not wash and cleanse it. We need to be like those smooth stones. We need to rest in that continual washing of God's Word, gaining purity of heart and becoming smooth and clean; effective warriors in our spiritual battles.

Leah lived a life filled with the giants of addiction. The giants kept her from living a victorious and successful life. Now, she is being washed by God's Word and is becoming an effective weapon in the kingdom of God. Instead of being saturated in the world system, she is now in a place where she is given life and the power of God is living in her. The cleansing and refining process can only happen by the Word of God washing us. That washing process is a daily transformation that turns us into effective spiritual weapons. Leah's daily process of refinement may take time and requires steadfastness and patience from me, as her mentor. As part of the process of refinement, Leah submits to my guidance and I hold her accountable. Her being washed by the Word will bring correction and character refinement. It will mold and shape her into an effective weapon for the kingdom of God. The Word not only promises her a life of freedom, but brings deliverance from the bondage of sin and fear that plagued and paralyzed her all her life. Just as David's life was saved from the giant and an army captivated by fear was delivered, Leah was delivered from a life of sin and is also able to stand in victory in the face of her giants. If we have an open heart, we will be smoothed and cleansed by the washing of water, the Word of God, and that will slowly remove the tarnish from our lives.

Another aspect of the cleansing process is that it can only be accomplished by the truth of His Word. As Leah's mentor, I fed God's Word to Leah daily, immersing her in Gods truth. Because of the cleansing of the Word, His image is starting to reflect from her with clarity. Now I'm starting to see the light of God illuminate from her to a lost and dying world. By looking at David's stature and physical ability, he was in a place of great vulnerability because he had no armor and essentially no protection. His protection, his true weaponry, was beyond what anybody could see. He knew the love of the Great Deliverer would faithfully take him to that place of great victory. When David boldly declared the Lord would deliver the giant into his hand, he also said that he would strike him and take his head off. If David had merely verbalized those words, it would have never taken David to that place of victory. Having a heart after God and knowing the Great Deliverer ensured David's great victory. He knew God loved him enough to stand in the middle of his battle and bring deliverance and freedom to him and his people. David had a personal relationship with his deliverer. In his heart he knew the love of the Father and stood firm in God's faithfulness.

When we face our giants without our weaponry of smooth stones—without cleanliness and purity—our words become empty, insignificant, heartless, and powerless. But when we face our giants as warriors of the Spirit of God, we can declare victory through Christ. Our hearts must be filled with God's love, and our lives need to engage in the Word of God to ensure we can possess that place of victory. David knew God's love; he was secure in his victory; he knew in his heart it was imminent because of what God had promised him.

Let's look at the promises of God and how they have affected our lives. When a loving father promises his child something, the child trusts the promise will be fulfilled. The father makes the promise and the child will anticipate the fulfillment of the promise because she trusts her father. If we place our trust in God and allow His Word to speak to our hearts, our destiny and purpose will be revealed. In that place of trust, we are promised victory in the face of our giants. We can stand in battle knowing we are covered and equipped with the greatest offensive and defensive armor life can offer, and that is the Spirit and the Word of the living God. In that armor is the Father's love and we are assured that we are able to walk in victory against giants. Those giants will be defeated because of the love of God that has been placed in our hearts. Through

God's love we are able to face these giants that have taunted and plagued us our entire lives, and because we know our deliverer personally, we are ensured a great victory.

My desire is to have a heart after God, for Him to anoint me with His love, and to be cleansed and purified by the washing of His Word. No matter what giants I've had to fight in the past and will fight in the future, I am clothed in His armament, adorned with His righteousness, and I'm assured that He will be there to help me conquer the giants that try to steal God's purpose and plan for my life. Don't be misled to believe that once you come to Christ you will never have giants to fight. You will have to face giants in life as Leah does. She continues to fight her past and our future involves fighting Satan, the pursuer of lost souls.

I know Leah's heart longs for others to see her without seeing her past, but the reality is that only God sees us as clean and pure. In your life you may have fought many giants or are still fighting them, trying to free yourselves from the bondage of past sins. Rest in the fact that your heavenly Father is there waiting to fight your giants and deliver you to victory in your life. My prayer is for you to have a heart after God like David. I am in pursuit of that very thing, a heart that beats compassion and is pleasing to Him at all times—a heart in pursuit of Him, one that is not divided, shows purity and follows and hides in His Word at all times.

LOST SHEEP

Or imagine a woman who has ten coins and loses one.
Won't she light a lamp and scour the house, looking in
every nook and cranny until she finds it? And when she
finds it you can be sure she'll call her friends and neighbors: Celebrate with me! I found the lost coin! Count on
it—that's the kind of party God's angels throw every time
one lost soul turns to God.

Luke 15:8–10 (MSG)

I must admit I did not want to pursue spending time with Leah
at first. Her life was not something that was attractive to me, but
over time I started to see her heart and need. God planted a purpose in me to reach out and rescue her. Pursuing a lost sheep can
be adventurous to say the least. When I learned what Leah had
lived through, the love of the Father emanated through me, and my
compassion and love for her grew. My desire was to save this lost
sheep and bring her into the fold of the flock for safety, healing and
restoration.

As a lost sheep, she wandered aimlessly from God. The only
way for her to return to the flock was for the Good Shepherd to
seek her. He needed to find her a shepherd, and I was chosen. I
knew she was lost and not able to find her way home. She was out
pursuing the pleasures of life, which gave her no promise of rest
and peace. I knew she was running and searching to the point of

exhaustion, helpless and hopeless. In my heart, I knew the Good Shepherd desired to take her into the safety of His sheepfold, and I needed her to understand that in her heart.

Jesus had pursued Leah all her life, just as He pursued or continues to pursue you. When we read about David, we learn the value of the one lost sheep and his willingness to search for that lost sheep until found. The one lost sheep is of great value to the shepherd, just as lost souls are important to God. That has to be the priority in our lives: to become a shepherd and go after the one lost sheep.

Sheep are not smart animals; they lack contentment and seem to stray easily. Sheep never know their destination; they wander off by themselves and very easily lose track and get separated from their flock. Sheep don't know to find their way back home again. There is no other animal that has less sense of direction than sheep. They will scurry and wander bleating and startled until the point of exhaustion because they never rest while being separated from the flock. They will continue on the move until they die of exhaustion. Sheep will never return on their own, the shepherd must seek and find them.

In Luke 15 there is a story of a woman possessing ten silver coins. One day, the woman lost one of the coins so she swept her house, searching with a candle, until she found it. After finding the silver coin, she called her neighbors to rejoice with her. This story is similar to that of the lost sheep. The woman who lost the valuable silver coin searched until she found it. The story is also indicative of Leah, who was lost, and someone needed to search to find her.

To God, Leah's soul is just as precious and of great value as the silver coin was to the woman who lost it. The important thing to know is this: Just because the silver coin was lost didn't mean that it had no value, and just because Leah was lost didn't mean she had no value. When the coin was lost, it was of no use until it was found and returned to the rightful owner. Leah, while lost, was of no use to her owner until she was returned into His hands. Sometimes we won't find a coin that is lost right away, and while it's lost, it sits collecting dust and becomes corroded. The image on the coin becomes obscure, almost unidentifiable. While she was lost, Leah collected the corrosion of the world, and her image became obscured.

Silver is a very sensitive metal that becomes dark and indistinguishable when exposed to the elements. Our human spirit is like silver. It is sensitive and becomes obscured when we are exposed to the corruption of the world. None of us can yield our intended return until we are returned to our owner, our Creator. Finding Leah and keeping her free from the elements of the world has been trying and many times frustrating. When I first saw her I really didn't see any value in her, but God revealed to me that she had value just like the lost coin and needed to be brought home to her original owner.

We need to put on the coat of the Shepherd and go after the lost sheep. We need to be willing to leave our flock, our comfortable lives, and our place of safety to go and bring home that one lost sheep. When we find it, we need to love and nurture the one lost sheep back to a place of safety. Let's be as the woman who searched endlessly to find that lost coin. Let's bring the lost coins back to the refiner to remove the tarnish of life that we may find their true value. I know my calling is to bring lost coins to their original owner and my spirit intercedes for clean hands and a pure heart. Personally, I found it required losing myself and focusing my constant love and attention in order for restoration to come to the lost treasure. Are we willing to give up our lives and dedicate ourselves to whatever God has called us to do for that one lost sheep or lost coin? I know that's what He has called us to do—die to self so others can live.

FEAR VS. FAITH

Give thanks to God—He is good and His love never
quits.

1 Chronicles 16:34 (MSG)

Let's talk a little bit about our past and see how it affects how we
live our lives. When we come to Christ, the blood of Jesus demol-
ishes every past sin; every act of rebellion and disobedience are forgiven and forgotten. The Bible tells us that if a man puts his hand
to the plow and does not look back, he is fit for the kingdom of
God. That means that once we come to Christ we shouldn't look
back to our past; if we do, we cannot move forward in what God
has for us. God puts promises in front of us, great and precious
promises that hold a future and hope for us. In order to succeed in
life, we must keep our eyes fixed on the future of those promises. In
other words, we cannot drive our automobile safely to a destination
with our eyes focused behind us. But if our eyes are fixed forward,
we can safely navigate the car to its intended destination.

If our eyes are fixed on a past that is filled with guilt, shame, and
condemnation, the future and the hope of God's promises will not
be obtained. Fear is paralyzing, but faith drives us with assurance.
The fear of our past can keep us from moving forward. Have you
ever had a dream in which you are being pursued by something evil
and being so gripped with fear that you could not scream or run?
If fear would have gripped David as he stood in front of Goliath,

he would have never been able to conquer the giant. Stories have been told of runners in the lead of a race who have turned back to look for the placement of their competitors only to lose ground and lose the race they had been leading. If our eyes turn back at a past that is forgiven, we will miss the promises of a future that is set in front of us.

After David killed the giant, people surrounded him and sang his praises. His victory was great, but his great victory was preceded by a great battle. In order for us to have victory, we must fix our eyes on the promise. Killing the giant was a victory that only David could see with eyes of faith. We need to understand faith will always demand a response from us. If we believe something so strongly in our heart, but don't act on it, then we will never gain victory in that situation. David said he would kill the giant, and the faith in his heart demanded that he respond. Leah had a life full of disappointments and defeats. Her life had come to a place where everything she ever had was lost, and even her own life was fading fast. Her life was full of defeat and hopelessness was overtaking her. There were no victories in her past that could make promises for her future, so her future held no promise and no hope.

When hopelessness sets into our life, our spirit man will not thrive, and our inner man will die. The hopeless person will give up, desiring not to live anymore. In that situation, the adversary Satan has won, and we've been defeated. Hope has to be imparted into the spirit of man. Without hope, death will win over the promise of a life of victory. The deception of hopelessness will rob us of every promise that God desires to plant in our heart. When Leah decided to turn her hopeless heart to God, the *zoe* life of God began to transform hopelessness into hope, and death into life.

The love of God is so incredibly deep it can brand and transform any hopeless heart. Cattle branding is the mark of ownership. The brand is deep in the skin, tattooed into the animal's hide, and can never be removed. The branding of the love of God cuts deep to the heart tattooing us, promising us hope and a covenant never to be broken. Leah's heart was once encapsulated with death and despair, but it is now branded with a future and hope. As she continues her new walk, God will give her greater understanding of His love. Trust will be built and the walls that guarded her heart from the possibility of hurt and pain will slowly dissipate. That love allows God greater accessibility to her heart. As the light of His love starts to take residence there, every form of bondage must vacate the dark recesses of her heart.

For instance, we reside in a house and we choose whom we allow into our homes. We will only allow some people access into the common areas of our home. Those we trust more we will allow into our more private areas. It is our choice because it is our residence. In the physical body our heart is the most private room in the house. We choose to whom we allow access. Some of us have had relationships in which certain people we thought could be trusted defiled the private room of our hearts by forcibly entering into our secret places. That won't happen when we allow God into our most private areas of our hearts.

God is a gentleman. It is important to know He will never defile the private room of our heart and never forces his way into those secret places. He will only access those places we invite Him into. He is not like many men some women have known. God won't lie to us, and there is no evil in Him. God is the most faithful lover you will ever know. He tells us to come close to Him, and when we take that step, He will come close to us. In order for God to do that, we must willingly give Him access to the secret places in our heart. When that access is given to Him, then the light of God will pour across our heart to destroy the hidden darkness. Darkness can only leave when light dissipates it. The love and light of God will take residence there, and all the pain, hurt, shame, and guilt will leave, bringing us a hope and freedom like we have never known before.

Just like when we have a wound that heals, the wounds of our hearts heal also. Some wounds are superficial, healing more quickly, but others are deep, taking more time. The rate of healing is determined by our willingness to give God access. God's ability is only limited by our unwillingness to give Him that access. We must remember God is love, all-powerful, all-knowing and has no limits. He can only be limited when we limit Him and we limit Him because of a lack of trust. Ultimately, a lack of trust is a lack of knowledge of His love for us. Only when we fully begin to understand the width, depth, height, and length of His love will we be willing to give Him full access. Giving God that access will bring a fullness of healing and create a well of hope in the depths of our hearts. When love and hope are deeply seeded in our hearts, we can pursue the giants that come at us, take back the authority they have had over our lives, and destroy them.

When David killed the giant, he didn't just leave him for dead. He wasn't satisfied until he had cut the giant's head off because the head is a sign of authority. David wanted to remove any authority the giant tried to have in his life. As we allow God to take residence in the secret places of our hearts, He will expose the darkness. He will bring death and destruction to those things that are darkest in our lives. As the giants fall, we must remove their authority from our lives just like David removed the giant's head. If we don't remove their heads, they are able to rise against us at another time and try to destroy us again.

The Word of God tells us to submit to Him and resist the devil, and the devil will leave. The giants in our lives will be stripped of their strength and place of authority as we surrender all to God. At that point of complete surrender, we can stand in the face of our giants and have the ability to stand against them, and they will leave.

When we submit to God we are submitting to His Word. Without the knowledge of the Word we gain no knowledge of Him. We will never know true deliverance nor walk in complete freedom without the knowledge and understanding of the One who is love. The One who imparts hope into our hearts. It is a true freedom that only the love of God can bring. The thing is, our hearts truly long for that pure love, deliverance, and complete freedom. They long for God's branding of love and the peace that walking in His love will impart.

There are two voices that direct us and drive us in our life. We are driven by the voices of either fact or truth. Fact is of the world, and it tells us what it can offer us. Truth is God's love and what is revealed to us through His Word. When we give complete access to Him, He rejoices in proving to us what His truth is. Truth will bring life and freedom to those of us who only knew the facts of the world. In gaining freedom we will gain knowledge of Him, and at that point, we start to understand what is required of us as His children.

Many of us will encounter a person who has been wounded by life's battles. Know that it will take perseverance and determination to feed them enough Word and truth to keep their heart longing for more of God's love. It is an exasperating experience at times to entice new converts to something they cannot tangibly touch or feel. The new life change and hunger will start by introducing them to God's love, His unconditional love. The true test of commitment to the new convert is the constant direction and attention that you will need to give them to help them succeed and walk in their new life and their new hope of love. Always remember His love is never ending and never failing, and we are called to do the same.

SURRENDER

The sacrifice you desire is a broken spirit. You will not
reject a broken and repentant heart.

Psalm 51:17 (NLT)

God's love is like the waves of the ocean. His love is consistent,
unwavering, and never ceases. We know the waves of the ocean will
always be there, and no matter what the situation, the love of God
will always be there too. God's love is unchanging no matter what
we walk through in life. His love is always there and it pursues us.

Picture a rock that has been in the ocean along the shore. The
waves roll into the shore bringing in barnacles and other sea creatures looking to attach to something. Over time, the rock, once
smooth and polished, becomes covered in barnacles. Its main iden-
tification is everything that has adhered to it.

Sin adheres to us and, in a sense, covers and encapsulates the
heart. The more sin to which we are exposed the harder our hearts
become. There is a point of revelation that has to be reached in our
lives, and that is the point of sorrow and repentance. We need to
understand that we will need a "higher" intervention to remove the
callousness around our hearts from sin. When we finally reach the
point of sorrow and cry for deliverance, God can intervene. When
we look at ourselves honestly and arrive at the understanding that
we need deliverance, then we are ready to meet the deliverer. It's

a realization we all need to arrive at: God is the only one who can take us to that place of freedom.

We become slaves to whatever and whomever we submit our lives. Sin constantly beckons and appears attractive, but the end result is the same—death. Sometimes, we can temporarily mask the hurt and feel good for a season, but sin is not the promise that will give us a better life, nor the freedom that God can bring from the bondage of a worldly lifestyle.

Many of us spend our lives pursuing the wrong things. We have been raised in an environment that tells us to attain success, find true love and accumulate wealth and riches of the world. We focus on the things we desire most. If we focus on things that are not godly, we can become a slave to them, and eventually they will destroy us. All of us become a slave to the things we pursue. If we pursue riches, we become a slave to work or the attainment of wealth. If we pursue greatness, we desire people to recognize us for that, and we become slaves to it. God's only desire is for us to have a heart after Him. Our pursuit should be the things of God. Things should never be elevated to a level where we are slaves to them. Our elevation should come only from accomplishing godly things. When we pursue the things of God and make right choices in our life, we will obtain the promises of God. We will never be in bondage or held in the grips of sin if we allow our spirit to find Christ and pursue true freedom in Him. We need to surrender to the things of God and quit striving for the things of the world. Remember, our pursuit is in the things that produce eternal value, not earthly value.

No matter what we've been enslaved to in our past, God paid the price to purchase us back from the slavery to which we sold ourselves. The price He paid for us was costly; a price we could never afford to pay for our freedom. God gave up His Son who was willingly sacrificed as payment for our freedom. The only requirement on our part is to accept the sacrifice, the free gift. All you have to do is surrender your heart and life to Christ, willfully acknowledging that He died for the sin and shame of our ways. In essence, just lift up your arms and say, "Okay, God, I'm guilty. I take full responsibility for being so stupid and ignoring you when you were always there protecting me and watching over me. I can't clean myself up, but I yield to you and really need your help." At that point of surrender and confession is where God's redemption and forgiveness kick in. You were a prisoner of your own making, now you are able to walk into freedom at no cost to you.

SECRETS OF THE HEART

And He said to me, It is done, I am the Alpha and the Omega, the Beginning and the End. I will give of the fountain of the water of life freely to him who thirsts.

Revelation 21:5–7 (NKJV)

Have you ever gone through your refrigerator and found food that had been forgotten or buried somewhere either intentionally or unintentionally? Maybe a leftover sandwich that was left in a lunch box or food shoved under the bed by a child. After a while, some of the food leaks a rotten odor and some would never be exposed unless we accidentally found it. Things that are harbored in dark places can breed bacteria. Darkness harbors certain creatures that thrive in the absence of light. In contrast, human beings left in the dark without sunlight will develop rickets, a disease in the bones due to a lack of Vitamin D. Light breed's life. My all-time favorite portion of the Bible is when Jesus talks about light and tells us darkness can never overtake the light.

If a person is placed in isolation or in a dark place for an extended period of time, eventually, that may drive the person crazy. Isolation—being by ourselves—can do the same thing that being in dark places can do. It causes the mind to harbor things that breed instability. I was a stay-at-home mom when my children were very young and I felt I needed to get out of the house almost daily to get relief from the isolated busyness of mother-hood.

Satan's sole motivation is to isolate people who once dedicated their lives to worldly living from the very thing that can bring wholeness and deliverance to them. He isolates them by keeping their minds desiring worldly things that mask the need for God. In addition, by masking people's need for God, the ability to search deep into the depths of their being is compromised. When people are isolated and saturated by the world they lose the ability to see what their original purpose and plan is. Satan will also isolate by speaking lies, telling us that a life dedicated to worldly things is sufficient. Pain and hurt are definitely products of sin and worldly living. They cause a person to build walls around themselves and withdraw, eventually not caring about things they should really care about.

When we were created, God placed a desire for eternity in our hearts. Man is a three-part being made up of spirit, soul, and body. The spirit man is eternal, never knowing an end. Our soul, which is our mind, will, and emotion, will also live eternally with our spirits. Our flesh, as we live in it now, will cease to exist when we die. The spirit man that lives within our physical bodies is the very core of our being and actually is more real than our flesh, since it exists beyond this life. There is an inner longing within our spirit for something beyond the life we live now. Eternity is in our hearts and our hearts long for something greater than life. Living in the isolation of the world can mask that longing, and Satan delights in that. That isolation keeps us from tapping into our spirit man or inner being. We live in a two-dimensional world and are confined to the boundaries of it by our flesh. We long for something beyond the confines of our flesh and the world in which we live. There is something greater and more powerful that we don't find in the confines of our worldly isolation.

Have you ever tasted chocolate of high quality from Belgium or Switzerland and noticed the difference between what you ate and the imitation? There is a huge difference between the two. Because you've tasted the best, the imitation chocolate doesn't satisfy. But if you've never tasted the real thing, then you think the imitation is real chocolate.

Most of us know there is only one Creator who created all things. There is one God and only one way to Him. There is only One who is omnipresent or everywhere at all times; One who is omnipotent, or all-powerful; and One who is omniscient, or knows all. That real God desires to rescue us from our isolation. His desire is for us to realize the condition of our hearts and what we have done to destroy the person He created us to be. When we arrive at that realization, the confines of the walls of isolation we lived in start to crumble and the darkness that covered our hearts dissipates. It dissipates because we are allowing the light to come in where only darkness existed. When we surrender our hearts and decide not to walk in sin, our spirit man can soar. Our hearts become illuminated by His light and Satan no longer has a foothold on our lives. We have found the real thing, and no longer will we continue to search or be a slave to the isolation of sin.

We will all face darkness at times even after we come to the saving knowledge of the Lord. Satan doesn't stop scheming ways to isolate us. Our only source of power is the light we hold in our hearts. Remember, darkness can't exist if light is there. Satan can't hold us in dark isolation, but delights in knowing our weaknesses. Just because a person becomes a Christian doesn't mean their battles with darkness will cease. Satan will fight to lure them back into worldly ways by dangling the fun times in their face. He masks the pain of the sordid past by making the isolation and darkness look exciting and fun. He wants believers to forget the loneliness and overwhelming emptiness of their past. We forget about the hopelessness we felt when we thought we were with someone we loved and they left us. These thoughts are tools the enemy uses against us. Satan's goal is to get us to forget who we are, what we are about, and what our purpose in life truly is. If we choose to live life with God, we will no longer live in the isolation of the dark walls of the prison of isolation; no more feelings of hopelessness because the darkness has left.

When we give in to the desire for eternity, we gain a new life, new light, and new purpose. We are able to walk in freedom and light, able to fight the darkness with light in our hearts. When feelings of hopelessness and isolation start to come over you, speak His name and darkness will flee! You can call on the One who is all-powerful, all-knowing and all-present. You are now able to walk with the Almighty at any time of the day or night. He will never dangle your past in front of you, and He will always be there to love you no matter what. God is the only one in your life that will love you unconditionally and always lend a listening ear. You will never walk alone or be alone ever again. That is the purpose of possessing eternity in your heart.

RELIGION VS. RELATIONSHIP

The life you see me living is not mine, but it is lived by faith in the Son of God, who loved me and gave himself for me. I am not going back on that. Is it not clear to you that to go back to that old rule-keeping, peer-pleasing religion would be an abandonment of everything personal and free in my relationship with God? I refuse to do that, to repudiate God's grace. If a living relationship with God could come by rule-keeping, then Christ died unnecessarily.

Galatians 2:20–21 (MSG)

I was raised in a home in which every need I had was met; I knew I was loved. My parents' heart was to do their best for my three sisters and myself. I spent many days in church doing what religious tradition taught me to do. Tradition taught me to kneel before those small wooden crosses. The images I saw were of a sad-faced Jesus. When I stood in front of these crosses, staring at the suffering image, I focused on the drops of blood falling from His body; the small nails in His hands and feet; His head hung to one side; and that look of distress on His face was unforgettable. I would stand for a moment, drop to my knees, as my religious tradition required, and spend a moment in prayer. I never questioned it because that was what tradition taught me to do. As a ritual I would walk around the church looking at the images of the progressive death of Christ. I was obedient to the religious requirements, but each time I left empty and always feeling a lack of accomplishment.

Time after time, I would repeat the ritual, trying to fill the emptiness I had inside. I would go into a building trying to find something real, and all I saw was this Jesus, suffering and defeated, hanging on the cross. My heart longed for something real, something greater than the depiction of the defeated Jesus. Not knowing what that was, I did the only thing I thought was right—I went back to the suffering image of the cross. But that did not satisfy that longing I had deep inside. My life was filled with perpetual sadness and all I could see was the pain and grief on Christ's face. My heart became heavy, because the only God I knew at that time was bound by nails to the cross.

Many think religion knows God, but religion has nothing to do with knowing Him. Religion tells us things we should do and shouldn't do in order for us to get closer to God. Religion dictated what I needed to do and gave me a false sense of security and confidence in being "okay" with Him. It never gave me a personal relationship with Him. What religion does is give us a false sense of security that keeps us from seeking that personal relationship with Christ.

Anything that separates us from God is wrong. Once I spoke with a prostitute about the truth of God's Word and invited her to church. She accepted and said she would bring friends, as long as I didn't tell her to stop doing what they do because that was how they made their living. I explained to her that anything that separates us from God is wrong. I may have never engaged in prostitution, but I did follow religious rules and regulations and that hindered me from having a true relationship with God. There is no difference in the sin of someone who prostitutes themself or in the sin of immersing oneself in religion. Either sin separates us from developing that personal relationship with Him.

We will never be able to leave that place of mere religion or sin until we learn to focus on Christ and depend on Him as the source for all our needs. God designed it so that if we commune with Him and seek that place of relationship with Him, then He will meet our every need. We can spend years sitting in the midst of religion, hearing about Christ, but a lack of knowledge of the truth will separate us from having a personal relationship with Him. It is not my intent to belittle the cross and what Christ did on it because without the cross we would never be able to have a personal relationship with the Creator and never find that true place of freedom. In addition to that relationship with Christ, we are able to find true victory and freedom at a place called the throne of God.

Without having that personal relationship our lives are like a person owing someone a large sum of money and not being able to pay it back. If the debt goes unpaid, the debtor would suffer great consequences. But if a trusted friend vows to pay the debt, the debtor trusts the friend will act on their commitment. The promise is made, but until the friend actually hands over the money, the promise is not fulfilled.

We all have a debt to pay because Adam and Eve severed their relationship with God by sinning. To renew the relationship with God required payment of that debt. Before the cross, the blood of a perfect animal was offered for the sin of man. It covered the sin only for one year, so the sacrifice had to be made again year after year. It's as if a financial debt had been paid, yet the same bill showed up in the mail a year later for life. The plan of God was for Jesus to pay the debt and be that sacrifice because He was perfect and without sin. The sinless life and death of Christ was the payment for the debt we owed for our sins forever.

Christ lived a sinless life, which qualified Him to become the perfect sacrifice. He went to the cross, suffered, and carried all the consequences of sin that we should have had to endure and placed them on His own body. If everything Christ did still hung on the cross, we would not be free. But after Jesus was crucified on the cross, He was buried and rose from the dead three days later, taking His shed blood to the throne to pay the price for our sin. The debt was paid and never again will it show up in the mail. None of us have to suffer the consequences of an unpaid debt.

So there I was as a child time and time again before a cross, never understanding there was anything beyond it or the meaning of it. I never understood there was a debt that needed to be paid for my sin and that someone paid it for me. I never understood that freedom was rightfully mine, and I didn't have to suffer the consequences of my sin.

Years ago my family took a trip through Europe. For most of the trip we had hotel reservations. But we had decided on being adventurous for a few nights and find hotels as we journeyed through other areas of Europe. We were on a train from Venice, Italy to Vienna, Switzerland. It was about nine at night when we found out the train was scheduled to stop around midnight at a border town in Italy and would not proceed toward Switzerland, our hoped-for final destination. My husband inquired about a place to lodge for the night. He talked to people working on the train who said our last stop would be a very small town and they did not think there was any lodging available there. So he inquired about staying on the train overnight, but was told passengers were not allowed to stay on the train. Getting on a train in a foreign country without prior hotel reservations was foolish; but not knowing our final destination was outright stupid.

That vacation experience reminded me of that time when I was a small child at the foot of the cross. I went to church without knowing what it meant or where that experience would take me. I was comfortable and confident of my life, but I was not really sure of my destination. The safety of the ride of religion pacified me, so that I could sit back and enjoy the ride, no questions asked. I was riding through life with partial information, but not enough to get me to my final destination: salvation through Christ.

Here I was in my early twenties, still wandering through life without knowledge of that final destination, until the train I was riding stopped at an unexpected destination. That "stop" ended up being a Christian music concert. When the music was over, the musician started sharing about Christ. He told about the suffering that Christ endured on the cross. He then spoke about a destination I had never heard about, a place beyond the cross. I had been on this journey through life, but I didn't really know where the train in my life was going to stop. All I knew was that I felt a false sense of security. The day the train stopped at the new destination I was told of something I had never heard of before, a place beyond the cross—that place of victory and freedom where Christ was no longer on the cross, but in a higher place. The image of Christ that I once visualized was no longer the image of Jesus suffering, dying and bleeding. I accepted Jesus Christ as my personal Savior; I now had a new image. That image was of a King who was victorious, who gave me strength and courage.

The simplicity of the message amazed me. All I did was believe that Jesus lived as a man, suffered and died on the cross, and rose again on the third day. Prior to praying that night I hadn't ever questioned my destination or my future. All I had was a false sense of security that I was riding the right train and it would take me automatically to where I needed to be. In an instant, truth was revealed to me. I remember asking myself, *Why hasn't anyone ever told me this before?*

I realized at that moment the information that I lacked could have destroyed me. I would have never made it to my intended destination—a place I like to call the throne or the place of victory. I now had the ability to approach the throne and commune with God. In life there is a right or wrong train to ride. Leah was also riding the wrong train in her life, and its intended destination was taking her straight to eternity in hell. If you don't have a personal relationship with Christ you are on the wrong train! We need to be riding the truth train that will take us to an eternity with God. A place of victory and freedom that is greater than anything you will have experienced in your life. It is not religion, but a relationship that is pure and filled with more love than you can ever imagine.

SEED OF PROMISE

Light-seeds are planted in the souls of God's people, joy-seeds are planted in the good heart-soil.

Psalm 97:11 (MSG)

Some children grow up in an environment in which parents praise them, while others grow up with parents that don't praise them. Some people grow up with a fire and passion to pursue everything that is set in front of them and some go through life with no real purpose and despise life. People whose parents praised and instilled a passion for life in them often grow up without many emotional needs. Those whose lives have not been nurtured may find other avenues and take to the things of the world for comfort and guidance. The way we were raised has a lot to do with how we learn to reach out and determines who we are and what we will accomplish in life. Many of us never realize that someone planted a seed and a promise.

Mary's promise was to become the mother of Jesus. Her sole purpose was to carry the seed of deliverance and salvation. It was a seed that needed to be planted in a place conducive to bringing forth life.

God's desire is to plant a seed of greatness in every single one of us, just as He did in Mary. He had our lives all planned out before we were born! In order for us to bear a seed of greatness for the kingdom we have to yield to His purpose and what He desires for our life. Before any of us can bear a seed of greatness we need to understand who Jesus is. Many people only know that Jesus was a great man. However, he is unlike any man we have ever known. He does not abuse, He is not angered easily, and He is not harsh. He will never be forceful and push Himself or His plan or purpose on us. He is truly a gentleman.

What we need to understand is every single one of us possesses the potential to carry greatness. But, none of us can carry greatness unless we yield our lives fully to Him. God would have never placed His seed in Mary without her yielding to His will. She had the free will to choose whether or not she desired to carry the seed of greatness, just as we have to answer our call.

In some religious cultures, Mary has been prayed to, idolized and even worshiped. God's intention was not for a vessel, or the carrier of the promise, to be worshiped. His intention was for the seed of promise she carried, the Messiah, to be the only One worshiped. All Mary had to do was yield her will and her heart to God. She knew in her heart that what she carried was of greater value and of a greater future. Some do Mary a great injustice by idolizing her because the motive of her heart was pure when she spoke the words, "Let it be according to your word."

Mary didn't necessarily see the value in herself, but she saw and knew the value in the seed that she carried. She knew that yielding her will, her desires, and her vessel was vital to carrying the seed of promise for the salvation of all. Just as Mary was chosen and set apart to carry the seed of promise, we are also chosen and set apart to carry our seed of promise. The world waited for the promised Messiah. They knew He was the One who would bring hope in the midst of hopelessness and life in the midst of death. God is searching throughout the whole earth to find people whose hearts will be loyal to Him. He is not looking for the top model, best actress, or the most intellectual. He is looking for you, a willing vessel who will say, "Let it be according to your word."

Some have a tendency to spend their lifetime with their eyes fixed on those around them. Some desire to be as beautiful as the magazine cover girl, as talented and gifted as the idolized actresses, or as intellectual as the last self-made millionaire. Our eyes are fixed on qualities the world holds at such high value. We seek, long, and strive to become something the natural eyes of the world can deem valuable. When we continue to seek value in the things of the world, the corrosion from that lifestyle will continue to cover who we truly are. We become tainted by things that appear to be valuable according to the world's standards. These things possess no eternal value and are not lasting.

When Mary gave birth to her seed of promise, shepherds went to Bethlehem to see Him. The angels announced to the Shepherds the Messiah had been born in Bethlehem and that they would find a baby wrapped in swaddling clothes lying in a manger. The Bible says the shepherds would tell everyone what the angel had told them concerning this child. Everyone who heard the shepherd's story marveled.

When the shepherds came to see the Christ child, it was Mary's opportunity for stardom. Everyone would know that she was the chosen one and how much she had endured to become the carrier of the seed. She endured the torture of the gossip, looks, stares, and being an outcast in society for not living and abiding by the law. The torture of the nasty looks and comments were not only directed at her, but at her family as well. Today, that would be a great opportunity for an interview on national television or have someone write a book about her. Instead of desiring fame and fortune, Mary kept all these things hidden in her heart.

Mary had that loyal heart God needed. The purity of heart, a heart that might have said, "I know it will not be easy. I will probably endure mocking from people around me, maybe even those closest to me, and I know I may be tempted to think I am all that and more because You chose me. But, God, I will do what you ask me to do, and I ask you in return to help me to stay humble. Help me not to be taken by the things of the world and the things around me. Help me to trust that You are the One who so precisely hand-crafted me and alone can keep me shined and polished." Imagine, Mary probably wasn't voted most popular in her graduating class or most likely to succeed. She wasn't offered college scholarships because of any great abilities. She just had a loyal heart, a willing spirit, and that is what God looks for in us.

Her seed of promise was physically manifested when she gave birth. Jesus was the seed that became a physical being. There is something much greater than the physical aspect of Jesus. Mary gave birth to a seed that was spiritual and divine. The infant to whom she gave birth would offer freedom and deliverance for all.

Just as He did with Mary, God has placed a seed of promise in every single one of us to birth something great. That is the purpose in us. The longing and desire of our hearts should be to tap into the true fulfillment of the promise in us. Fulfillment will never be known until destiny and the purpose in us unite within the heart. At that moment the purpose of life will be unveiled and hope will carry us through to victory in our destiny.

There are many people in this world who have natural abilities that everyone presupposes will lead to greatness. But natural abilities can be to a person's detriment. When people rely on natural abilities, they never move into anything greater than themselves and have no desire to produce or birth a God-seed of promise. When people possess greatness, others are patting them on the back all their lives for being so naturally wonderful, and they are never able to tap into the true vision that is in them. These types of individuals often carry themselves into self-destruction because they never find the fulfillment their inner heart is searching for. Sure, they will find self-gratification, but there is no true satisfaction, and their heart remains empty and constantly searching to satisfy that longing. Our hearts long and cry out, but nothing satisfies the deep longing. The real voice in us is never found, and the seed of promise that was planted is never unveiled. Some of us go through life as average, always longing to be greater. Many of us look at those with natural abilities and gifting and long for what they have, thinking that it will bring contentment and fulfillment into our lives.

In Genesis, Abraham questions God's promise because he is childless and has no offspring. God tells him to look at the stars and says that's how many descendants Abraham would have. God reiterated that Abraham would have children, but ten years passed and still no children. Sarah, Abraham's wife, being seventy-five years old, questioned if God's promise would ever come to pass. So Sarah decided that she was going to make it happen herself. She tells Abraham to go to her maidservant Hagar and have sexual relations with her in order to have children by her. Hagar becomes pregnant and then gives birth to Ishmael. Ishmael was not the child that God promised to Abraham. He was a counterfeit and ultimately brought grief to Sarah. Sarah took matters into her own hands and did not wait for the promise of God, so there was no true fulfillment from Ishmael's birth. The real promise that was to come to Abraham and Sarah was a boy named Isaac, but he would not arrive for another fifteen years.

When we sell out prematurely or chase after worldly promises, we bring grief and problems into our lives. There are women I know who possess greatness within and a desire to tap into the goodness of it. They cautiously wait for the manifestation of promises in their lives and know there is a destiny to obtain. There is a glimmer of a vision in each of us—even the lost—but the glimmer shines dimly because the reality of life sometimes snuffs it out. That glimmer may be dimmed by a loved one or anyone who seeks to fulfill his or her own agenda causing the glimmer of a seed of promise to fade. Deep inside, we hold on to the hope and tell no one of our discouragement for fear of losing that little seed of promise. The corruption of discouragement will repeatedly cover the vision in us until our glimmer of hope turns to hopelessness. At that point, hopelessness takes over, and death appears promising. The enemy uses deception to pull the hopeless into the lie, telling them a better way would be to totally give up the promise inside and let hopelessness have its way.

The problem arises when we place our trust in worldly systems or in people who may betray us and we naively become entangled in bondage after bondage until we are engulfed in complete hopelessness. The elements of the world cover the heart until we feel there is no hope and have no feeling of security. Finally, the corrosion that covers the purpose God originally gave us will snuff out the little promise of a future that will give us life. Satan is the master of darkness and his entire purpose is to get us to lose the original image that we hold in our hearts. Once we lose ourselves and become entangled in his bondage we will stay lost and never fulfill our true purpose and destiny.

You see, life is like a child who plays hide-and-seek with her father. The small child giggles as she hides, fully expecting to be found. The point of the game is to hide and not be found, but what the child really longs for is to be found, picked up, and embraced by her father who seeks her. In the depth of our heart, all of us are created with a longing to be embraced by our heavenly Father. We long for His eyes to fix on our hearts and change our lives, but instead we play a game of hide-and-seek. What we pursue are things that appear desirable to our eyes. Even though our heart was created to long for our heavenly Father to find us, our flesh enjoys hiding in those worldly desires and we continue to sin. We continue playing a game of hide-and-seek until we reach the point where we truly desire our heavenly Father to embrace us.

The goal is total submission of the heart. When you allow the Father to embrace your heart and remove the shame and unworthiness that years of worldly living and desires have caused, then that glimmer of a seed of promise will start to shine through. It is at that point you can start living and benefiting from the blessings and promises God has for each one of us. The seed in each of us will start to sprout and grow, and we will see evidence of the darkness diminishing.

As we submit our hearts and desire to have more of God, He starts the process of removing all the guilt and shame we caused by indulging in the pleasures of the world. A desire to possess clean hands and a pure heart is what He delights in and should be our ultimate goal. The more we desire Him and allow Him into our hearts and lives, the more we are able to see our true promise and purpose. It's the promise of life without darkness, hopelessness, and longing. The only longing we will have is to draw close to the One who saved us from the grips of darkness. For those of us who have lived a sordid past, there will be such eternal gratefulness; in turn we will love much, desire to do His will at all costs, and give birth to our seed of greatness.

NO HOPE

For nothing is impossible with God.

Luke 1:37 (NIV)

Have you ever been to a place in your life where you felt there was no hope? Maybe you believe you're too tainted and weary. Many of us have wondered if we should hope for a better life. Do we wait and hope to see something good come to pass in our lives? Do you wonder if you possess any purpose in life or if it's too late for you? There is a story in the Bible about an old couple named Zacharias and Elizabeth. They had been married for many years and had no children because Elizabeth was barren. For years they had hoped to produce a child because one of God's blessings are children. But they never saw the manifestation of a child after trying to conceive for many years. Being barren and old is a pretty hopeless situation.

Zacharias was a priest in the temple. Every year, he and Elizabeth would travel to the place of worship where a lottery would select which priest would put on the robe of righteousness. One year, Zacharias was chosen. When he went into the inner chamber, an angel appeared to him and told him, "Do not be afraid because your prayer has been heard. You and your wife will have a son, and you are to call his name, John."

In the middle of hopelessness, despair and barrenness, God will always be there to intervene, and the impossible is replaced with the possible. Elizabeth conceived when conception seemed impossible. When things appear hopeless you need to know that with God nothing is impossible! God heard the prayers of Zacharias and their hopelessness was replaced with hope. Please know that God always hears the cry of the heart that longs for hope and purpose.

The process of birthing hope and purpose is like a fetus developing in the womb of a mother. The child needs nourishment for a healthy birth. So it is with our every dream and passion—proper care and nourishment is needed so it may come to fruition. Proper nourishment comes from the Word of God and the life He gives us.

God will always place people around us who will speak life to the dreams in us. On the other end of the spectrum we can be assured that the enemy will always make sure to send people who will speak death and try to use them to abort the dream within us. We need to be as a mother who protects the fetus inside her; we must always protect the plan and purpose we carry inside us at all cost.

During Elizabeth's pregnancy, Mary, the mother of Jesus, who at the time was pregnant with the Messiah, went to visit Elizabeth. Her purpose was to confirm Elizabeth's promise. Elizabeth was pregnant with John, the forerunner of Christ. It was God's plan that not only would Mary bring confirmation to Elizabeth, but Elizabeth would confirm Mary carrying the Messiah. God will always bring "Mary's" into our lives to speak life to our dreams. He will bring the "Mary's" to us and that still, small voice inside will let us know He sent them. Likewise, we will know the impostors who are sent by the adversary, those who come to speak death over our dreams. The naysayers who come and speak doubt and unbelief must be silenced and dismissed in order for us to give birth to our promise. The important thing to remember is the Spirit of God always brings life and never death. Our promises require much care, endurance, and patience and when that vision comes alive, there is no greater satisfaction than knowing that with God nothing is impossible. God is faithful! His love will never disappoint and when we delight in Him and are obedient to His call, His promises always come to fruition. We need to learn to speak to the vision within and watch our future blossom as a flower in springtime.

RUN AND NEVER QUIT

Do you see what this means—all these pioneers who blazed the way, all these veterans cheering us on? It means we'd better get on with it. Strip down, start running—and never quit! No extra spiritual fat, no parasitic sins. Keep your eyes on Jesus, who both began and finished this race we're in. Study how he did it. Because he never lost sight of where he was headed—that exhilarating finish in and with God—he could put up with anything along the way: Cross, shame, whatever. And now he's there, in the place of honor, right alongside God. When you find yourselves flagging in your faith, go over that story again, item by item, that long litany of hostility he plowed through. That will shoot adrenaline into your souls!

Hebrews 12:1–3 (MSG)

The Bible says that to everything there is a season, a time for purpose, a time to be born, and a time to die. Leah was born into the world at a specific time with a purpose. Before her creation ever came into existence, the appointed time of birth was set aside for her. Every day of her life was already planned out with a vision of her God-given purpose and destiny.

During her lifetime she lived a hard life; a life plagued with much illness and many failures. As a young adult, she had already contemplated in her heart that she would probably die young.

Because she dabbled in sin and lived a worldly life, she lost her vision, purpose, and the fight to live out the rest of her life. She lost the vision of the race she was set in life to run and over time decided to quit the race before she even started it.

Originally, her job was to run the race and compete to accomplish what God had placed in her and run it with endurance. From the beginning she chose to run her own race and failed. But since she has become a child of God, He is now in charge of her life and has set her on a path to obtain His promises. She is learning to run the race day-by-day with endurance. I am running alongside her, making sure to encourage her to fulfill her purpose and destiny. Right now, her goal is to focus on the race ahead and be driven by the force of the purpose He placed in her heart.

Her past was full of sin, but now she is covered in righteousness. Living a sinful life weighs us down, and we carry a load that is too heavy for us to compete. After we come to Christ, the weight of sin is removed, and we are covered in righteousness. Righteousness can be compared to the attire worn by competitive runners. The competitive attire is made of a special cloth and can be compared to an outer layer of new skin. Runners wear this to decrease the resistance from the wind. If believers are clothed in righteousness, they are in a place of right-standing with God, and the resistance and weight of their past is significantly reduced. They can now run the race with greater force; the bondage around their heart has been released! Jesus knows our future and has set our race in life. When we run the race in obedience to His word, we are promised abundant life, health, and wholeness in our spirit, mind, and body; we will lack nothing and miss nothing.

Our purpose is to be runners in a race competing for a prize. If we possess a purpose and compete, we are able to set ourselves on track to pursue our call and plan. So it is necessary, as believers, to participate in running a race while keeping in mind that our ultimate goal is to obtain the final prize of fulfilling our destiny and purpose. The Bible tells us we need to get rid of the weight we carry from life and the sin that so easily ensnares us and to run our race with endurance.

There is no such thing as a one-man party, and this race is not a one-man race. It is a relay race that we are to run with others. True victory is being able to run the race with a team of believers who are set to rob death and hell of its victory. At the end of the race, there is a prize of eternal life that we are given, and we have an assurance that victory is secured if we always run with Him. The prize of victory is eternal life. While we run this race, we possess the ability to conquer our fears and destroy all bondage. All of us must run and not grow weary and never lose heart. We must possess a level of hope that abounds in the heart to secure the victory that has been promised to us.

There are many times in life in which we will experience weariness that can bring discouragement and hopelessness. Even though we experience these feelings we need to press forward and pursue the prize that is in front of us. Participating in a physical race requires that runners exercise and push their bodies to their physical limits at times. That can bring great pain and certain muscles in the body can experience great fatigue. It requires every muscle working together well to run a race. It also requires all members in a body of believers encouraging and edifying one another to finish the eternal race. What it takes is all of us working together to ensure every believer completes the race in victory; having no injuries or even casualties and no one exalted above the other. That is what mentoring a new believer is. Recognizing that none of us have attained perfection, but if we press on to finish the course together, we can finish what has been put before us. Every part of the physical body is important when running a race and every member that is part of a spiritual body is of great value in the race of life.

While running this race of life, many of us will suffer wounds. In order to survive these wounds, it is important to secure a connection to a life source, and that is Jesus Christ. It is a life source that is vital to fulfilling the promises of God. We can compare the need for a life source to a limb or extremity that has been wounded in battle. So badly wounded that there is little blood flow or life left in it, and without proper care, the wounded limb can become necrotic and die, needing amputation. On the other hand, if the body part that was wounded is properly tended it will heal and become a productive member of the body, easing the load off of the other areas that have compensated for the loss. Initially, the wounded extremity that is healing will not effectively carry its share of the weight. The other members of the body must help carry the weight during the retraining process. That's what it takes to run the race, every Christian helping others to be strong, training them, and assisting them in completing the race. The whole body of believers should carry the wounded until healing starts and wholeness is evident.

Restoration is the process that brings wholeness and should never be despised. Its purpose is to bring about great beauty to the new believer just as the butterfly emerges from its cocoon. The butterfly starts out life as a caterpillar and is entombed in a cocoon, just like we are entombed in our sin prior to salvation. Having an encounter with Christ is like morphing from a caterpillar that has been entombed and emerging as a beautiful butterfly that flies with purpose. While in the cocoon, it needs to be nurtured and cared for until it emerges from its tomb of bondage and matures into the beautiful butterfly that brings beauty and has a purpose in life. We are like caterpillars entombed in sin and after finding Christ, we are able to emerge as beautiful butterflies moving on to free others from their tomb of life.

As Christians, our call is to bring wholeness to everyone we meet who is wounded. It is our job to bring the wounded to the saving knowledge of Jesus who frees them from their cocoons. There are times when it is necessary to continue to run the race right next to the newly-saved. Helping them mature and grow until they are spiritually fit enough to run the race on their own. Part of the maturity process is assisting in removing the "old" body and transforming the "new." That process is sometimes tedious and painstaking, but proper care will ensure those we are called to mentor finish the race they started. All of us have a promise if we finish the race, and that is an eternity with Christ.

The promise I received for Leah was that she would be fully restored. The Master created her, but it is the responsibility of the body of Christ to bring restoration to her. I know her life was so mercifully pursued and is now being miraculously transformed. I can personally tell you there is great joy in watching a life restored, watching her grow and be transformed, equipped for victory, running her race with endurance.

VISION

I say this because I know what I am planning for you, says
the Lord. I have good plans for you, not plans to hurt you.
I will give you hope and a good future.

Jeremiah 29:11 (NCV)

Several years ago, I knew a wonderful woman. It appeared to me
that she had everything to live for, or at least that's what I thought.
I knew she held on to a longing in her heart that her husband
would one day come to know Christ. Her desire was for him to
know the love of Christ she had experienced in her life. She cried
out to God for his life day in and day out. The longing she held
deep in her heart appeared out of reach. As the years went by, the
hope and dream of him knowing her Savior were prolonged, and
her heart started to lose hope in God's promise. When hopelessness takes root in our hearts, the heart becomes sick and loses its
purpose to thrive. Hopelessness opens us up to many elements,
one being illness, an attack on the body that many can't fight. This
woman became gravely ill and she came to a point where she felt
she had no reason to fight to live. Death draws near, and the idea
of spiritual peace becomes better than the desire to live. None of us
have life without a purpose or a dream. In this case, hopelessness
encapsulated this woman's heart, and death was ready to take her.
The day she died, I vowed to fight to spare others from death and
hopelessness. That is why I determined to fight for Leah. I chose

to fight for her because death wasn't an option. I longed to see the purpose and destiny God planted in Leah revealed.

Author Helen Keller said, "The only thing worse than being blind is having sight but no vision." The society we live in is driven by physical senses. Many don't realize the impact our physical senses have on our decisions and ultimately our destiny. Leah is severely hearing impaired. She reads lips extremely well, and many would never know of her impairment. In fact, many have questioned her disability because of her ability to compensate with her other senses. For instance, we can both be in the same room, yet she will be more aware of her surroundings than I am. She is more visually in tune to things around her than I am. Leah lip-reads conversations that I am unable to hear and feels by vibration things I take for granted, like traffic going by or cell phones from a distance. She has been forced to adapt because of her disability. It challenges her other senses, and they compensate to a greater degree for the loss of hearing that many times it seems she has no impairment at all. The reality of it is that she is not the one lacking—I am.

When I think of Helen Keller, I don't think of her disabilities, but of her abilities and accomplishments. Keller lacked physical vision, but saw greatness from inside. She didn't focus on what she couldn't do, but on what she could do. I have discovered that true blindness is having no vision, and true deafness is having no voice. When there is no vision and no voice within, our outer physical senses will drive us. They ultimately will rule, reign, and navigate our lives.

We are led by what we see, hear, feel, taste, and smell. We measure fulfillment by the ability to have these five senses satisfied. If you ask someone how their day was, most of the time their answer will be based on how their five senses were satisfied. Our life journey is to satisfy these senses. We think the greater the fulfillment, the greater the success. The gauge of success in life is if our eyes can see pleasure and ears hear greatness, then we can attain everything we desire.

Society has promoted what our physical eyes like to see, setting the standard for which everyone strives. The greater the satisfaction to our physical senses, the greater the pursuit is of the things of the world. Life's goals are driven by the ability to satisfy those senses, and greatness is measured by attaining a certain level of that satisfaction. Images of the "ideal" person and the "ideal" life are presented to us continually on TV and magazine covers, tantalizing our senses. As women, we strive to attain that picture of a perfect person in fad diets, clothes, and haircuts. We feel that we fall short of those standards if the picture we portray is not successful or accepted by others.

Just because Helen Keller lacked physical vision doesn't mean she didn't know what true vision was. True vision is the drive and purpose from within that cannot be seen, heard, felt, smelled, or touched. It is a drive that pursues and persists in spite of what our senses dictate. Great vision will always encounter great resistance. Our natural senses can be the greatest enemy to fulfilling our God-given vision. Our greatest tendency will be to pursue the path in life that looks the most desirable, sounds greater, feels better, smells good, and tantalizes our taste buds. Our pursuit in life has to be from the vision that God put in us. Whatever it is, it should drive everything in our life. If God places a vision, a plan, and a purpose in us, there should be nothing that would stop us short of obtaining that plan.

Genesis tells a story of a young man named Joseph. Joseph was seventeen, and his father loved him very much. He honored Joseph with a coat of many colors, which signified that he had great favor with his father. Everyone knew that he was the favored son. His outward attire gave the impression that everything was going well for Joseph. He was the top dog, sporting that coat of favor. According to the world's standards he appeared very successful because of what he was wearing; however, they could only see what was on the outside. There was something about Joseph that no one could see from the outside. God gave Joseph a dream and showed him a vision of his purpose and planted it in him. The dream God gave Joseph involved him reigning over his brothers and his nation.

Now a battle would begin to steal the vision that had just been planted in Joseph. He would face opposition that would try to tear him down and steal the vision in him. While he was having the dream, the vision was being burned into his heart. Joseph became firmly grounded in the dream God gave him. Dreams that are from God are spiritual experiences that are placed deep in our hearts, never to be forgotten. The test of time would tell if Joseph really had embraced the dream. Sometimes, opposition will attempt to take that dream or vision from us. But, the very dream that the opposition comes to steal is the same dream or vision that will sustain us through all that happens over time.

There is one important thing to remember, that every opposition that can come against the dream and vision will do so. If the attraction to the desires of the world does not draw us away from the dream and vision, the world will pursue us with a vengeance in order to steal it. That is what Satan does. He presents things to draw our attention away from the dream and vision God placed in us. There are people who spend their lifetime pursuing fulfillment from the world who will never live the dream because their senses and desires are satisfied with things from the world. On the flip side, there are people who are firmly grounded and desire to live out their dream like Joseph. Worldly things attempt to steal our dream. Time will always reveal if we truly embraced the dream that was placed in us.

God-given dreams will always extend beyond self and beyond the satisfaction and fulfillment of our own desires. Trying to fulfill the dream will always bring opposition, the greater the dream, the greater the opposition; the greater the opposition, the greater the opportunity for victory.

Joseph woke up from his dream and decided to share it with his father and brothers. How they envied him. You will never pursue a God-given dream without resistance, and those who you think would be your greatest fans will probably be the ones who give you the greatest resistance. We could all learn from Mary, even after she gave birth to Jesus—who was the dream in her—she kept all the things she heard from God and pondered them in her heart. In other words, there will always be people that will try and kill your dream. Remember, Samson shared all that was in his heart with Delilah and when she had the opportunity she stole his dream. Samson's desires caused him to sell out and his dream was forfeited.

Every God-given dream will always seem to be bigger than what we are capable of handling. Pursuing the dream will require that we deny every personal desire, while causing others to envy us and possibly sell us out. The people who sell us out do not realize that our dream could be their salvation and deliverance. The very thing they resist and try to kill might possibly be the very life they breathe. Joseph dreamed he would rule and reign over his brothers and save his people. Joseph's brothers were tending the flocks and his father sent him to make sure everything was okay with them. When his brothers saw him coming, they got together and conspired to kill him. They were laughing and saying, "Look, the dreamer is coming!" Originally their plan was to kill him and put him into a pit. Sometimes we think family or friends closest to us will be our greatest support, but they end up being our greatest resistance. When the dream possesses us, we will not be moved by people mocking us or trying to sell us out. It will not uproot the vision and there is nothing that will cause us to abort the dream that is deep within. Joseph's brothers did not know they were trying to kill the very thing that would sustain their lives in the future. Through all of this opposition, Joseph would have to see a greater purpose in his dream other than himself.

When Joseph comes to his brothers they tear off his coat. They were jealous of the favor the coat represented and thought if they stripped the coat from him it would remove the favor they saw on his life. When there is a purpose within, it brings us favor with God, and no one will be able to remove that from us. His brothers may have tried to strip him of his favor, but the dreamer will never stop dreaming. The brothers' plans shifted, and instead of killing Joseph they decided to sell him into slavery, hoping to stop his dream. Joseph was sold as a slave twice, and the second time he was bought by a man named Potiphar, an officer of Pharaoh, ruler of Egypt. The whole time Joseph was in slavery, God was with him. Joseph held onto his dream and vision and became a successful man; God made sure he was safe and prospered. Eventually, Joseph ended up in the house of the master of Egypt.

Joseph was sold into slavery twice and ended up becoming a servant in an Egyptian's home. Joseph was a successful servant, and everything that was charged to him prospered in his hands. We need to remember the bigger the dream, the bigger the resistance; the greater the battle, the greater the opportunity is for victory. At this point, many of us would have given up on the dream because the resistance would have been too much. No matter what Joseph encountered, he was never moved by what he saw, heard, or felt because he remained focused and stood firm in his dream. Once God gives you something He will not take it away. No one can take it from us unless we forfeit it. It is like a covenant. When God makes covenant with us, He will never break it. We decide to walk in the covenant relationship or to break the covenant relationship.

Everything is going well for Joseph in Egypt. He has been appointed the manager in Potiphar's house, and he is keeping watch over everything that belongs to Egypt. All of this success didn't go to Joseph's head because he realized his dream was bigger than anything he would desire in life. He was dedicated and obedient in denying every personal and physical desire.

Before long, a huge distraction was presented to Joseph. Joseph's master's wife came to him and tried to seduce Joseph into having sexual relations with her. At that time, Joseph was seventeen, and his hormones were probably raging. That type of offer would be difficult for most men to turn down. But Joseph was loyal not only to God, but to his master. Joseph remembered that if he pursued this avenue, he would be fulfilling his own desires, and it would put his dream in jeopardy. Joseph recognized there was greater purpose in his dream than fulfilling his own physical desires. The master's wife tried to lure Joseph by tantalizing his senses. Her purpose was to steal the dream from Joseph, and he knew it. He rejected her offers and because she was disgruntled she retaliated and went after Joseph. She took a piece of his garment and told her husband that Joseph tried to sleep with her. His master was angered and had Joseph thrown into prison. Things were not looking so good for Joseph again, but we know that truth always prevails. Even in slavery, Joseph knew God was with him and had shown him great mercy.

Joseph was in prison, but prison didn't have Joseph. Joseph became friends with the prison keeper, and in spite of his imprisonment, God was going to make sure his dream stayed alive. The prison keeper gave Joseph charge over all the prison. In time, Joseph started interpreting dreams. Now Pharaoh's baker and butler were also put in prison because of some sort of wrongdoing. While there, both had dreams and didn't understand what they meant. Joseph heard about the dreams, knew what they meant, and told them he could interpret the dreams for them. After interpreting the butler's dream, Joseph asked the butler to remember him and show kindness by sharing Joseph's story with Pharaoh. The butler agreed and ended up going back to work for Pharaoh. One day, Pharaoh mentioned to his butler he had a dream and didn't understand the meaning of it. The butler remembered that Joseph interpreted his dream, and it came to fruition, so he told Pharaoh about Joseph. He had Joseph brought to him from prison to tell him what his dream meant. Joseph did, and Pharaoh valued Joseph and made him ruler over all his land. He gave Joseph the highest level of office in all of Egypt.

During the time of Joseph's ruling, the dream he interpreted for Pharaoh came to pass. There was a drought in the land, and famine set in, but because Joseph was faithful and stored goods away,

Egypt didn't suffer from the effects of the famine. The Israelites, however, did suffer and Joseph's brothers came to Egypt to ask for food because they were starving. They had no idea the brother they sold into slavery years ago was now ruler over Egypt and would decide whether they would live or die. During the years Joseph was in slavery, he never stopped thinking about his father. He desired to see his father, and this was the opportunity to do so. Remember, Joseph's dream was he would rule over his family and save his people. His brothers came in to ask for food and did not recognize Joseph. Joseph knew who they were and demanded to see their father and little brother. He would then reveal himself to them. Joseph brought deliverance to his family and people!

Joseph could have taken on a victim mentality and become disgruntled and offended, but bitterness would have never produced the greatness that came out of Joseph. When we pursue something greater than ourselves, distraction, and trials will come and try to get us off course. Satan doesn't want us to hang on to our dream, because when we do we are able to rule and gain authority and favor in everything we do in our lives. Sometimes resistance may cause us to cast off the dream. We can choose to either become the victim or the victor. The thing we need to keep in mind is the bigger the dream, the bigger the battle, and the bigger the battle, the bigger the victory.

God will always make a way when everything seems to be impossible. When we look back at Mary and her story, we remember the vision she was given was to carry the deliverer. The angel assured her that with God nothing is impossible. Mary and Joseph hung on to their dream and remained faithful to their call. They never compromised and never aborted their dream, no matter what the opposition was. In spite of every problem or situation that came against them, they stayed faithful and determined to carry through. Their responsibility was to guard and carry the dream they were both given. They hid it in their hearts and cherished it until it was time to give birth to it.

Many of us might think we could never survive all of the opposition that Mary and Joseph encountered. That is because many of us have never been able to remain faithful to what God has given us. We have led lives of compromise and long ago aborted our dreams. Some might believe they never had a dream to begin with, but that is not the truth. Before we were even created, God placed a plan and vision in each of us. A dream and vision that He expects us to carry out to fruition. Once we come to know Christ, the plan and purpose and vision is ignited. At that point, we can either choose to follow it and ground ourselves in it or abort it. We can either choose to be like Mary and Joseph or be like Samson. Mary and Joseph dug in and made it happen; Samson sold out cheap.

Are you willing to see your plan and purpose come to fruition, or are you going to sell out cheap and abort your future? Are you going to allow the trials and problems to sway you and keep you from accomplishing the dream and vision God has for you? One thing we need to remember is, that no matter how bad we have messed up, God can always restore the dream. If we place our trust in Him, our dreams and visions will never die. If we choose to walk our own path and fulfill our own desires, we will abort the plan and purpose of God; it is our choice. We are never too lost for God to help us find our way back. He will always be there to guard and protect the dream and vision He placed in us. He will be faithful in creating a path that can bear the opposition and attack of the enemy. During those times of attacks and opposition, the one thing to remember is we must continue to hang onto that dream because He is always faithful and keeps His promises.

PLACE OF FREEDOM

Not by might nor by power, but by My Spirit, Says the
Lord Almighty.

Zechariah 4:6 (NIV)

When we yield our lives to God, He is able to fill us with the greatest power we have ever known. The Bible tells us the same power
that raised Christ from the dead lives and dwells in our mortal
bodies. God is omnipotent or all-powerful. As children of the
Most High God, we have access to that power source and can plug
in at any time. Possessing that power and not utilizing it as God
intended is like having a house full of electronics and power tools
and never plugging them into electrical outlets to use them. They
are of no use if not plugged in, but when they are plugged in, they
draw from their power source and become useful for the purpose
for which they were made. It is necessary to plug into the power
source that is available to us so we can become effective tools for
the kingdom of light.

Let's talk about the difference between kingdoms. There are
two kingdoms, one of light and one of darkness. Both possess the
power to conquer, but one conquers by destruction, the other by
love. One power source oppresses, the other edifies. We choose
which power source we want to possess and what kind of life we
want to live. When we do, His Spirit manifests His power in us and
through us to be able to live a victorious life. It is a life that won't be

without hardship or problems, but a life that can have victory and peace in times of trouble.

We can pursue peace all of our life, but without the Prince of Peace in our lives, that pursuit is futile. As children of God, His peace abides in us and is at our constant disposal. He is the giver of wisdom; when He abides in us, wisdom is ours whenever we want to access it. He is the Helper; when He abides in us, He is ready to help us through any circumstance. He is the comforter; when He abides in us, He is ready and willing to comfort us through every trial and tribulation. These are the blessings we are able to enjoy as children of the King: power, peace, wisdom, help, and comfort.

If we don't possess peace, then are we able to offer another person peace? There are many counterfeits that promise help, peace, wisdom, counsel, and even freedom. A counterfeit bill appears to have value and may even yield some benefits, but eventually, it will be identified as a counterfeit bill and ultimately destroyed for its lack of value. Every counterfeit promise that offers us peace, wisdom, counsel, and freedom will eventually be exposed. The spiritual counterfeit is Satan, and he has control over the kingdom of darkness. True freedom is Christ; He lives and dwells in the kingdom of light.

Leah, once void, searched for peace in the empty promises of the counterfeit world consisting of drugs, finances, and superficial relationships. All of these counterfeits promised her peace and appeared authentic and valuable, but over time, failed to produce what was promised. The counterfeit promises of the world only delivered destruction. She searched for wisdom in higher education because she felt it was the only means of bringing her true fulfillment. The false promise was that if mainstream society valued it, then she would have attained a level of wisdom that would bring her fulfillment and acceptance from others.

There is no true fulfillment in worldly pursuits. However, there is a choice outside of the worldly system that will never disappoint or destroy. All we have to do is ask, believing that we will receive this fulfillment and power that comes from knowing Jesus Christ. It's a power source that will bring healing, freedom, and deliverance to a lost, hopeless, and dying world. This power is available for any follower of Christ willing to know Him and desire it. Those desiring a pure source of power can't purchase it or earn it. It's a free gift given to us by the grace of God. It's one of those blessings that we don't deserve, but because of God's great love for us, He pours out this gift on us.

The ultimate purpose of the power is for us to be able to offer freedom to others and deliver those needing the chains of bondage broken off their lives. Every chain, bondage, and yoke can be broken under His power and will bring freedom to the captive. We must believe in the ability of the Spirit of God to break and destroy every yoke and bondage. We must believe in the power source in us, and desire that others be set free. We have to ask ourselves, if we were in a burning building and others' lives hinged on our ability to remove people from that building, would we flee and save ourselves, or would we risk our own lives to save others from the fire?

The eternal pit of hell is very real, and some people live hell while on earth. They see death as freedom from their hell in this life. They possess no knowledge of hell or refuse to believe that the eternal tormenting fires are real. Through His empowerment we possess the authority to break the chains of hell, allowing God to impart hope into the hopeless by bringing to them freedom and deliverance.

There was a man who loved us in the middle of our rebellion and sin. The man who sacrificed His life is the One that reached His hands down into the burning fires of hell freeing us from the consequences of our rebellion and stretched out His arms on a cross. He endured the shame of a humiliating death by allowing himself to be nailed to a cross with every one of our sins.

While Jesus was on the cross, God could not look upon Him because of the curse of sin He carried, but because of Jesus' great sacrifice, God can now look upon us as sinless. The Spirit of God took the lifeless body of Jesus and transported Him to the gates of hell. The purpose was to set the captives free and because of that, we too, possess the power to free others from hell. Before we come into a relationship with Christ we are captives who need to be freed from hell. Remember Leah and the life she searched for? Well, God gives life to her and a promise that He will breathe His breath into her daily; promising her a life of freedom and victory. Because of what Christ did on the cross we have a Savior who sees us as pure and clean. There is no remembrance of the things we did in our past and there is a promise of a new life and a clean slate. Our promise is that we will know true love, security, and peace. God's promises are true, and He is faithful and just to forgive all. All we need to do is yield to Him and receive pure and undefiled peace and love.

Most women have envisioned a brave knight in shining armor or a gallant prince. Most desire a love story in which they live happily ever after. But there is only one true knight and one true prince and that is Christ. Only His love is able to see beyond all past hurts and pain. His love was a perfect love that hung on the cross to offer us salvation and peace. That is the only love story ever written that will carry into eternity. What it gives us is a peace and love the world cannot offer. The world's peace is a counterfeit and has no lasting value. The only thing that has value is salvation. Know there is the peace of Christ that passes all understanding.

REFINING FIRE

For you, O God, tested us; you refined us like silver.

Psalm 66:10 (NIV)

After Jesus' resurrection, He commanded His followers to stay in Jerusalem and await the promise of the Father, God's Spirit, who would become their source of power. That source of power would enable them to become effective witnesses for Him, performing signs, wonders and miracles. In our modern age, we comprehend natural sources of power and appreciate the use of electricity. But when it comes to Christ, we have a tendency to reject the ultimate power source that is available for our lives to work properly and effectively. It's not tangible and we cannot see it, But if we ever tap into the reality of that power, it would be undeniable. If we don't plug into that power source, our lives will lack vitality and real purpose.

Jesus relates the power of God to fire. He is a fire that refines and purifies. The Bible tells us that He will sit as a refiner and purifier of silver. When a silversmith holds a piece of silver over fire and allows it to heat up that is called the refining process. While refining the silver he will hold it in the middle of the fire where the flames are the hottest. The reason it has to be held in the hottest part of the fire is to ensure all the impurities are burned away. He has to be careful not to leave it in there too long, so the silversmith holds it and keeps his eye on the piece the entire time it's in the fire. If he leaves the silver in the flames a moment too long, it will be destroyed. How does the creator of the piece of silver know when it is fully refined? When he sees the reflection of his image in it!

Can any of us see Christ's image in our lives? When I met Leah, she lacked the image of her Creator because she never yielded her heart and life to the Refiner, allowing Him to take and refine her. There was no image of the Refiner because the sin she participated in had covered and tarnished her life. When we don't yield our lives to the Refiner, our bondage is imminent, and we will lead lives of destruction. If we yield to Christ, our ultimate source of life, and are willing to place ourselves in the refiner's fire, we will find true love and freedom. Our bondage will be released, and the fire will refine until the Creator's reflection is revealed. Just as the silversmith sits and watches carefully, God will watch us and wait not a moment too long until our transformation can be completed. It will only happen if we yield completely to Him. At that point, our lives will reveal His saving grace so those around us will see the transformation of His work. The refining process is difficult and tedious, but it is worth the heat of transformation to remove those areas of impurities we haven't allowed Him to have. When we decide to give our lives totally to Him, He is able to perform and create His best work of art. We are that piece of art that will reflect the Refiner's image and shine for all to see. Reflecting Christ's image—Christlikeness—is our ultimate goal!

FIRMLY PLANTED

And he shall be like a tree firmly planted and tended by
the streams of water, ready to bring forth its fruit in its
season; its leaf also shall not fade or wither; and everything he does shall prosper and come to maturity.

Psalm 1:3 (AMP)

When small children are learning to gain independence, they are
determined to do things without assistance. A preschooler will
repeatedly say, "I'll do it," in hopes of accomplishing their task
without any help. As parents, we know the maturing process is cru-
cial for normal and healthy development. We desire for our children to be independent, but we stand close by in case our child
needs assistance. We will verbally encourage them in hopes they
can accomplish the task they set out to do. That is what our heavenly Father does for us. He watches, waits, and is always standing
by to encourage and rescue us if we fall.

A small immature tree planted in the soil has a narrow and a
shallow root system. For the tree to survive the elements it must be
girded between support structures to prevent the wind from blow-
ing it over. Otherwise, it may not withstand the elements and eventually die. The wind may blow and storms may come, but the tree
will be safe because the supports are firmly placed next to it keeping
it safe. Girding structures allow trees to grow thick and strong. As

the tree grows and the root system goes deep, the more secure it will be in its soil.

When Leah was transplanted from bad soil conditions that were of the kingdom of darkness into a soil that girded her in the kingdom of light, she started out very small and immature. She was vulnerable to the elements of the world from which she was removed. God knew she needed girding as a small tree, so He knit her to a person who would guard her while she became firmly grounded in the soil of the kingdom of light. The word of God will cause her roots to grow deep. Hopefully, that grounding will prevent her from being uprooted by the tumultuous winds of life again. The winds of the world will try to make her waiver. The pressures of the familiar things of her past will try and press her, in hopes of causing her to buckle under pressure and fall. Satan's purpose is to uproot her from her new source of life. Satan is waiting and watching our every move. He is waiting for the appropriate time to attack and come in for the kill. God always knows what we need to survive the storms of life. He brought to Leah someone who would offer protection and girding through her growing process. My calling is to be spiritually knit to her, and to gird with love, but I am to challenge her as well. If times get tough for us and the storms of the world come at us, God has people He will place around us who will never give up on us.

While we are in the process of girding someone, the important thing to know is that a commitment needs to be made to them. They need to know the person God has sent will be consistent and is someone who will stay with them through all their trials and troubles. They need girding and protection until they mature and grow. We aren't there to judge, but to lead and guide, because it is the Word of God that will chastise and bring correction. If she didn't have someone to protect and gird her, the winds of her past would have uprooted her and would have caused her to fail. Now, because she is being girded, the winds of her past have little or no effect on her. Of course, it is still our responsibility to stand by while the newly planted trees are maturing and growing. We are called to guard and protect them in case the storms of life become too much to handle. We never want to lose a tree that has been planted in the kingdom. It is our responsibility to mentor, guide, direct, and discipline. Trees are pruned to produce strong, healthy, attractive plants. This delicate work of removing branches one at a time is the same as a mentor applying discipline to a new believer. It enables them to grow and blossom, eventually seeing fruit, so we can reap a harvest.

We need to learn to nurture and care for one another. We are not in this fight for ourselves, but for people who need to be planted in the kingdom of light or kingdom garden. If we don't tend to those newly saved individuals, the storms of life and the elements of the world will destroy them giving Satan joy over those lost souls. Let's learn to be gardeners in God's kingdom and gird those who are young in Christ so they are able to grow strong and carry on their call.

ILLUMINATION

But their evil intentions will be exposed when the light shines on them, for the light makes everything visible.

Ephesians 5:13–14 (NLT)

There is a light that is ready to illuminate those who sit in the shadows of darkness and death. In darkness there is hopelessness. The shadow of death is a heavy weight on our physical body. How could anyone reach for light when their strength is all gone? If somehow they could muster just enough strength in their heart to cry out, they would find the One who is able to illuminate their darkness. There needs to be a desire in each of us to reach for life beyond the force of our own darkness and despair.

A young man at my church told this story about his life. He had been running from God for years, steeped in sin. As he lay in a prison cell, the voice of God spoke, "When are you returning to Me?" He responded, "I will not, Lord." The voice cried out again, "When will you return to Me?" At this point he suddenly felt paralyzed and weighted down by the power of God. Not only was he locked in a physical cell, but bound in a spiritual cell as well. It was a cell of death and bondage that he had created because of destructive decisions and worldly living. In prison, there were no distractions, no longer able to run, he lay paralyzed on a bed of hopelessness only able to respond verbally to God's plea; still, his response was, "no." His only options were: turn his life back to the One who created him or die. After twelve hours of battling in his heart, the pursued finally answered the pursuer, "I will return to You." At that moment, the prisoner was freed from the cell of bondage that held him spiritually. Even though many of us have never been in an actual prison cell or had an experience like this young man, we all live in our own prison of sin and need to be delivered from our cell of bondage.

Hopelessness keeps us living in the grips of death and it binds us in chains. Hopelessness is a condition of the heart in which the heart is transfixed into thinking there is nothing else out there. It is a place of discontentment with life and a disbelief that something can rescue us from that state. Leah had been searching for years to find that place of peace and contentment. There was a longing in her heart for something greater, but everywhere she looked and everything she tried was unable to fill that longing and void. After searching in vain, the longing turned to hopelessness. Where there is hopelessness, there is darkness, and darkness creates a hardened heart. She mentioned to me one day that she thought no one cared, and there was nothing that could change her circumstances. That is hopelessness. The heart accepts there is nothing to believe in, and it loses hope. Lack of hope leads to unbelief, and unbelief takes us to a place of hardness. Hardness lacks caring, which will eventually lead to death. There is such a darkness that surrounds the heart in that state of hopelessness there is no way for someone to realize there is light. We don't realize the light in our lives is from hope and faith. Jesus is the provider of hope and faith. When Leah was at the point of death, she told me she felt there was no turning back from that place of hopelessness and there was nothing to live for anymore. I felt that if I could plant a bit of hope and light in her, her heart would be able to see its way back to feeling. The Bible tells us that no one comes to the Father except the Spirit draws them.

Even a person who is lacking hope and is ready to die can be drawn by the Spirit of God. It is our responsibility to plant the tiny seed of faith into people that are hopeless. Tending to it and watering it will bring a growth of faith. With that in place, they will be able to see there is light in their dark place and begin to believe there is someone who truly cares. When the Spirit draws, light starts to illuminate and will expose the hopelessness. When hopelessness is exposed, the walls of the hardened heart will start to crumble, and His light will start to fill the empty, dark places with hope. The light of God responds and will illuminate the darkest places with only a heart's cry. He is ready to illuminate the darkness and fill the heart with His light. All it takes from the mentor is time and listening to someone's heart cry for the opportunity to plant that seed of faith. One seed at a time is all it takes to remove the hopelessness from a desperate heart and realizing that every seed we plant and properly care for will bring a harvest. We bring them out of their hopelessness by caring and getting them to realize that every decision they made in life, or will make, brings a harvest of consequence. Decisions made outside of the will of God will only start to bring back the hopelessness. Outside of His will, we have no promise. A good harvest comes out of walking in His will. There is a world of opportunity and choices that are presented to us in life. Weeds and seed are ensured to grow in the soil side-by-side. If the right choices aren't made, then the weeds are sure to choke out the good seed. The decisions we make can taint and tarnish our lives. Our job is to spread the message that the answer to bad decisions and destruction is illumination from the light of God.

Picture a one-year-old child seated in front of a birthday cake to celebrate her first year of life. Her fingers poke at the cake as she ponders whether to eat or not. Someone seated next to her assists by pushing the child's hand into the cake and guiding it to her mouth. The taste is sweet, but she is not enthusiastic to continue eating it. She tastes the frosting, but becomes distracted by the messy, dirty hands. Because she is a child, her mind lacks the ability to find a place to clean dirty hands. So she reaches down and wipes her hands on her bare belly. The sweetness of the frosting tempts her into putting her fingers back in the cake; now a dirty belly is smeared with frosting. The child doesn't like being dirty, but she has no ability to clean herself, and it becomes a vicious cycle. It is a sweet and innocent moment that is obviously harmless.

Many reach out for the apparent sweetness of life only to become covered in its dirtiness. Those around us prod us to eat of it, and then they gladly join in the celebration. The decision and choice is placed in front of us, and at that moment, we don't think of the consequences. The vicious cycle of tasting the delicacies of the world and the consequences of our tainted flesh is continual and eventually draws us to a point of hopelessness. When we get to that point we have no ability to cleanse ourselves and that is the greatest opportunity for freedom. We no longer can look to ourselves for deliverance and our hearts need to reach out to God. That cry for help allows God to pick us up and clean us off.

In the middle of our inability, the light of God becomes our ability, and He will illuminate our tainted lives. When we don't know how to clean ourselves, He is ready to do it for us if we ask. When we ask, we are opening our lives up for Him to work. The things that attach to us from a life of worldly living can't be removed from us unless we come to Him with an open heart. When we don't know how to unlock the prison doors or break the chains of bondage, all we have to do is ask. He is ready to unlock the doors and break off those chains. Immediately, the darkness will dissipate and life comes to the prisoner as the heart is illuminated. The prisoner who once sat in the darkness of his sinful cell will be released and a new path will be illuminated by His light. His light becomes a constant beam of direction guiding our feet on a new path, filling our empty hearts with hope, no more to be a hopeless prisoner.

MIRROR

Has anyone by fussing before the mirror ever gotten taller by so much as an inch? If fussing can't even do that, why fuss at all? Walk into the fields and look at the wildflowers. They don't fuss with their appearance—but have you ever seen color and design quite like it? The ten best-dressed men and women in the country look shabby alongside them. If God gives such attention to the wildflowers, most of them never even seen, don't you think he'll attend to you, take pride in you, do His best for you.

Luke 12:27 (MSG)

When we look in a mirror, we see our image, but over time, if we never looked into a mirror or saw a picture of ourselves again, the image of who we once were will fade from our memory. Also, our self-image can be influenced by people who speak into our lives. They may be people we see in our daily lives, or they may be people we read about in a book or see on television. Either way, there is a desire in our hearts to become that certain image that appeals to us. We are molded by what is put in front of our eyes, our ears, and our hearts.

All people have different personalities, characteristics, and moral standards. One person can bring about change in another, but only if that person has a willingness to change. Someone in the relationship will change over time, either becoming weaker or stronger.

When my daughter was a small child she would sit and watch a certain TV show. When she did, she would act like a bratty character in that show. Needless to say, that TV show wasn't allowed to be viewed in our home. The bratty character and her strong personality dominated my daughter's personality; it was apparently attractive to her. The show caused my daughter to mold her personality to the image portrayed by that character so my husband and I made sure that character no longer had a voice in her life. Because she was a small child it was important that our voice was louder than the voice of that character, not audibly louder, but louder as an influence in her life.

As parents we wanted to put in front of her eyes, ears, and heart a mirror image of what we desired her to become as she grew older, because one day she would mirror her image to others. Our goal was to produce a young lady who would project a desirable image to those around her. During our lifetime, many things will be put before our eyes and we will hear many things with our ears; many things will influence our heart. As we stand in front of the mirror of life, what will influence our lives and what image will we project to others?

Life is like an ocean, and we are like the beach. If you could choose which beach to be, would you choose a beach in Hawaii that has white clean sand and clear blue warm water? If you looked to the horizon, would you see clear blue skies? I know nobody who would choose a beach of tarry black sand full of seaweed, broken glass and debris washing upon brown, foamy waves. I doubt any would choose a horizon of gloomy skies with a view of a broken oil tanker spilling its nasty, gooey oil on the beach, with the oil sticking to the sand and everything else it touches.

Sometimes it seems life continually spews tarnish just as an oil leak covers a beach. A bird caught in the trap of an oil slick will attempt to free itself, but with every gooey wave, it becomes even more saturated with the deadly tainted waste. Any attempt to leave the place of destruction is futile because the weight of the destructive tainted oil permeates every fiber. The flight to freedom is no longer attainable; there is no hope of escape, and no hope for freedom from the deadly substance. When the bird tries to clean itself, it ingests the toxic substance, and death tightens its grip. The bird fights for life to the end.

That is what sin does to us. It is like the oil that tainted the bird and slowly destroyed and took it to its death. Sin will entangle our lives to the point where we are unable to see our way out of its entanglement. Slowly but surely, we lose sight of who we were created to be and the image we once saw in the mirror vanishes quickly. We look into the mirror, and all we see is a distorted view of what we used to be. We become steeped in sin and live life according to the world, participating in things that slowly cover and entangle us. We see no way out, and continue to fight our way through the sludge, only to become more saturated by the toxic substance. Hopelessness sets in.

We should be able to look in the mirror and see the image that Christ created us to be. Leah once told me that because she lived for so many years searching and reaching out to things that were not of God, that those things slowly engulfed her to the point where she really didn't even know who she was anymore. She lived a life hoping to attain the best, searching to fill the void, and trying to recreate the image that she once had. She mentioned to me when she looked into the mirror, all she saw was a hard-hearted, greedy person who hated life and wanted to die. She told me she felt her whole life had been a lie and was one battle after another; she was tired of fighting. Slowly, sin engulfed her and she realized it would be futile to fight to live.

Trying to live a good life without God is impossible. There is no such thing as living a good life if you don't live life to please God. We either live our life possessing Christ in our hearts or we don't. Living a "hot" life means pursuing your purpose and plan for

God; living "cold" is living the lie for the devil. God would rather you live for Him or live for the devil, but not both. The devil wants us to become so saturated in the toxic substances of life we lose the image of who we are. He takes the perfectly created image we used to see in the mirror and transforms it into a distorted image of what we used to be. Distortion happens because we can't see ourselves clearly in the God-mirror. Satan attempts to cloud the mirror and gradually pulls us away so our original image is gone. There is only one way to rescue ourselves from the tainted sludge of Satan, and that is to clean and saturate ourselves in God's light and love.

When someone has been so hurt and hardened by the ways of the world, it's hard to penetrate the covering of the tainted oil. The only way to rescue people in that condition is love, unconditional love. The God-kind of love that does not hold a person's past against them, the past of that tainted oil of sin in which they lived. We need to rescue them from that oily beach, grab them up, and start to wash the oil off to expose their original image. We need to take them to a place where they realize the need to cry out to the One who created their perfect image in their original mirror. They need to know that when we cry out for Him to be our Father, He will be there to embrace us with open arms. It doesn't matter how tainted or how covered in the muck we are or how sordid our past is. Our job is to fight the battle for them. They are so covered and tainted we need to be the light that leads them back to the Creator to find the image they lost. I fought a spiritual battle to get Leah back into the hands of the Creator. Starting to wash the muck and oil of her past was difficult, but worth the work.

When we take the time to lead someone to the Lord, there are rewards in that and the harvest is great. The end result is being able to watch their true image come to light. The exciting part for me was watching Leah come to the realization that she could live under the shadow of the Almighty and would find her image again. It's an exciting thing to help Leah find her way out of the tainted oil and muck of the world to a safe place. It's a place she never knew while swimming in the sea of her past. She never knew the arms of a loving Father who promised He would never leave her. I knew she had never known such love and making her realize it was available to her was a long and difficult process. The life she led was so covered and tainted and her original image was almost gone. Helping her find that love was amazing and rewarding. Walking through the mess and entanglements of her life started to capture my heart. The web of lies and traps set by the accuser to draw her away from the purpose and plan God had for her was almost complete.

I'm hoping you may put yourself in the place of Leah. Imagine yourself walking through someone's bondage, hurts, and pain. I know all of us have had those hidden hurts and pains deep in our heart that cover us in muck and tainted oil. It is a trap that is set to destroy us. My prayer is that you let this chapter speak to you. Stop and take a moment to look in the mirror and see which image appears to you. Is it the original image God gave you, or the image you allowed yourself to become while being covered in the tainted oil? If your original image isn't the one that appears, find a quiet place and ask the Father to come and remove the muck from your heart. Allow Him to come and cover your life and polish off the tarnish of the world from the treasure you truly are.

PREMATURITY

But his father said to the servants, "Quick! Bring the finest robe in the house and put it on him. Get a ring for his finger and sandals for his feet. And kill the calf we have been fattening. We must celebrate with a feast, for this son of mine was dead and has now returned to life. He was lost, but now he is found." So the party began.

Luke 15:22–25 (NLT)

Everything has a season, and there is an appointed time for every purpose under heaven. A woman who is pregnant will deliver a baby in due season. During the nine-month gestation there are many stages to her pregnancy. If a baby is born in the first trimester, the first three months of pregnancy, the infant will likely not survive. There is no viability for the birth, and death will follow. If the infant is born in the second trimester, the third to sixth month, the chances of survival depend on the development and maturity of the child's viable organs. The onset of problems after birth at this stage can be challenging, requiring care to increase the baby's chance of survival. In that case, intervention is required either short or long term. The infant may grow up to lead a healthy life without signs of prematurity at birth, or may grow up with lifelong challenges requiring increased care the rest of her life. Chances of survival vary according to the child's physical development. On the other hand, an infant who has fully developed for nine months typically requires no higher level of care at birth to promote its development and the child leads a healthy life.

I think that's what all of us desire in life, a life that will require no additional care. Sometimes life seems to be full of additional care: challenges, roadblocks, and obstacles. There is a story in the Bible of two sons. The younger of them asked their father for his share of their inheritance in advance. The father reluctantly gave him his portion of the inheritance knowing the son lacked maturity. After he received his inheritance, the younger son gathered all his possessions and journeyed to a different country. He wasted his inheritance, spending it all on friends, parties, and a lavish lifestyle. A recession developed and there was no more money to live on. He ended up finding work as a slave feeding pigs. He was so poor that he craved to eat the food he fed the pigs.

While he worked as a slave, he thought about his father's hired servants and how they had enough bread to eat while he was starving from hunger. He decided to give up what pride he had left and go back to his father and ask for forgiveness and tell him he was no longer worthy to be his son.

So he traveled back to his home and while he neared the house, his father saw him from a distance. His father missed him and compassion welled up in his heart, and he ran to embrace and kiss his son. The father told his servants to bring out his best robe and put it on his son. He also had them put a ring on his finger and sandals on his feet.

Because God's plan and purpose has been placed in each of us, every day has been ordained. In essence, God's perfect timing is in everything. The younger son in the story was ensured his inheritance, but he requested it before his season or its time. He was not at a maturity level to handle it properly, and the end result was the loss of all of his inheritance. Premature birth of a God-ordained plan can bring death to everything that could have sustained life.

That's what we do with our lives sometimes. We demand prematurely what is rightfully ours and the end result is the death of a promise. Prior to that death is the hurt and pain of impending loss because of wrong decisions. Actual physical death may not take place, but life continues empty and broken by shattered dreams. We end up with never-ending hurt and pain because our choice and decision was made out of season.

The younger son always thought about the life he left behind at home; always thinking about his error and his rebellion. He decided to return to his father and ask for forgiveness. It took a lot of humility on his part to go back. His repentance meant that he was sorry for his sin and rebellion. He owned up to the fact that the choice he made was a rebellious decision. The change of heart manifested in a change of action. Finally, he returned to his father, admitted the error, and submitted his life to his father's authority.

While he was gone, his father awaited his return. I believe his father longed for his return and had compassion for him. It was not the reception the son had anticipated because at his return he told his father he was no longer worthy to be called his son and requested to be as one of his hired servants.

Every single one of us, if we were honest, would have to say there has been some point in our lives in which we have given birth prematurely, in which we made a decision to do something outside of God's perfect will and perfect timing. Even those who grew up not knowing God have made decisions prematurely and out of rebellion. Perhaps many of the decisions we made were contrary to what our parents or authority figures advised us to do. Death of our purpose may not have come from that situation, but we definitely feel the pain and grief from it.

Our heavenly Father is like the father of the prodigal son. We make decisions to get our inheritance early, and we end up spending it prematurely. We end up making wrong decisions and bring trouble, unwanted struggles, and endless problems on ourselves. We bring unnecessary destruction to our lives, our family's lives, and our homes. When we step outside of the will of God, we open ourselves up for the enemy to come and steal our riches just as the prodigal son who squandered his inheritance because he left his safe place. He opened his life up to the enemy, and the enemy took him from a life of wealth to starvation and a life of slavery.

It is important to realize the enemy is standing by waiting for us to step out of the will of our Father so he can steal our plan and purpose. Satan sets us up for defeat and laughs at us when we fail, but God is gracious and tender in mercy, waiting there to rescue us from Satan's grasp. He is waiting with open arms to take us in and clothe us in His best robe, ring, and sandals. He is always there to embrace us in the middle of our failures and set us on the right path. He is willing to take us out of the pig slough and cleanse us so we can sit in a place of authority with Him.

PURITY

Create in me a clean heart O God and renew a steadfast
Spirit within me.

Psalm 51:10 (NKJV)

Leah had been saturated in a world system, but now she is called
of God. The vices of the world and her past constantly call her to
return to it. The life that had once been summoned by the world is
breaking free from its pull and is now being immersed in His love.
She found God after He had pursued her, her entire life. Once
being lost, now she is found.

I am able to hide and protect Leah by keeping her close and
in a safe place so she won't be drawn to her past. The ways of this
new life are so contrary to the world's way she is not used to it. The
fruit of change becomes evident everyday, now that she's living this
new way. Offering forgiveness to those who have offended you is
a difficult task. Her biological father verbally abused her. He used
words that conveyed his disappointment in her and those words
tormented her continually. Now her father is gone, but the memories of her childhood and unforgiveness linger in the recesses of
her mind. The hurt and pain was deep, the offense cut to the heart.
The Bible tells us that we have to forgive those who offend you and
ought to honor your father.

I knew her pain went deep, but I always knew the Spirit of God
would help her forgive. I explained to her that He would empower

her heart to change, but she had to confess it with her mouth and invite the Helper to empower her to forgive. I saw the encapsulating wall of her heart become pierced by the Word of God and I saw the forgiveness process begin. When Leah chose to forgive, the tears flowed unhindered and her grieving heart melted the anger and pain away. The chains of bondage of unforgiveness broke and the hurtful memories no longer torment her mind or pierce her heart. The unforgiveness that was in her heart is now shattered.

Alcohol and drugs were used to suppress the pain and unforgiveness. Now, instead of dulling the pain with vices, she is filling herself with the truth of God's Word. God is continuing to wash away the tarnish and the image of her Creator is starting to reflect from her. The image of a sordid past fades and the new image, the one she was created to be, can be seen. As we read the Word of God we can glean wisdom and counsel from it. It bears witness to the voice in us and will start to clean our hearts, causing the corrosion of our past to fade.

Her vessel is now being purified as she gains knowledge from the Word. The battle between the truth of God's Word and the lies about her past sin confront her. The vices of the past call to her pretending to be nothing but pleasurable and forget to remind her of the consequences that brought her to a place of death and destruction. The alcohol and drugs might have numbed and covered the pain and torment for a moment, but she will soon realize the Word of God is what will bring her lasting freedom. Satan's motive is to lie about the pleasure and self-gratification of that past. But when our spirit man becomes slowly strengthened by the truth of God's Word, we can find freedom. It's a truth that promises the captive to be set free of their past. It is a truth that promises us life and life more abundantly, not temporary fixes.

Being delivered from the pits of hell creates a love that longs to declare His love and goodness to anyone who will listen. Leah's desire is to share about the Merciful One who gave her freedom from the torment and bondage of more than twenty-seven years.

She knows the truth must be told and shared because there are many others who live life the way she did. How can anyone know such freedom and not share the truth with those lost, bound and dying? She has been transported literally from a world of darkness and hopelessness to a life of freedom. I know, and she knows, the battle is very real and our fight is for other souls. After my encounter with Leah, I wondered how anyone could stand by and watch as the enemy of death and hell swallows and consumes others who do not know the truth.

One of the most difficult things in life is learning to love those who hate you and persecute you. It is a difficult task and most of us wonder how it can be accomplished. But, there is a greater love that stands in the face of persecution. Life is not just about being delivered from the pits of hell, but about those who might hear of the truth and of its glorious deliverance and possibly believe. Our battle is not against people who hate and persecute us, but against the kingdom of darkness and hell, which desires to swallow us up and destroy us. Her previous battles in life were physical, but now Leah's battles are more intense because they are for other souls, not just for her. Love speaks loudly because it covers the sins of our past. It's that same love that drew her to Him and now draws others as well.

I have explained to Leah that our ultimate goal is to achieve clean hands and a pure heart. In order to do that, we need to draw closer to Him and allow His image to shine through us with more clarity for others to see. The Word of God is there to guide and direct and His light will illuminate our path. The walk of a believer is not always easy and is very contrary to the ways of the world. After I explained that to her, she realized none of us can commune with the Lord unless we possess a level of purity. We obtain purity as we hear the Word, obey the Word, and draw close to Him then His light shines in the dark places of our heart and will expose the darkness. Sometimes we will veer from His will and not heed His counsel by choosing not to forgive or retaliate when we are persecuted. Maybe we choose to hide the evils of our past in our hearts, but God knows they are there and we must willfully surrender them to Him. If we choose not to willfully surrender the hurt and pain, they will fester like a gangrenous sore. God's promise is that He will heal the brokenhearted, but in order for Him to do so the brokenhearted must yield their heart to Him. If we veer from the path of God's will onto a path of offense, unforgiveness, and rebellion it becomes a path that will pull us away from the truth and the light of God's Word. Our vessel will become tarnished, and the image of our Creator will start to fade. Our purity will be compromised and our ability to ascend to that place of communion with Him will be hindered.

When the Spirit of God takes residence in us, we become His temple. At that time we receive the precious gift of understanding of His Word. The Holy Spirit gives us understanding of the Word of God, to those who vow to commit to Him. Understanding and illumination of the Word is the greatest wisdom we could ever receive. If we live by the Word of God and receive wisdom it will bring us understanding of the promises of abundant life. It is like the soothing comfort of water to parched lips. Cool water is able to satisfy our thirst. The transition from the kingdom of darkness, hell and damnation into the kingdom of hope, eternal salvation, and abundant life can be compared to transitioning from a dry, desert land into a land of flowing rivers of living water. The only prerequisite to receiving the indwelling of God's Spirit is a willing and yielding heart that desires to have a relationship with Him. The indwelling of His Spirit is a gift of God, and there is not one person that is ever too tainted to receive that.

Let's talk about purity for a moment. Have you ever gone fishing and caught a fish already cleaned of its scales and guts from a lake or a stream? I would think not. The cleaning process takes place after we catch the fish and that is the same process as when a person comes to Christ. God cleans us after He catches us. None of us can ever be ready to stand in the presence of God by our own ability. It is only by the indwelling of the Spirit of God, the knowledge we gain from His Word, and the cleansing process—after we yield our hearts to Him—that He can indwell and change our lives. That act right there guarantees our freedom and a new life.

We obtain different levels of wisdom when we eat from the Word of God, and that wisdom will never be exhausted. Earlier, I mentioned a will or testament has to be read to know what has been bequeathed in an inheritance. The will in God's Word must be read in order to gain knowledge and understanding of the inheritance we have in Christ. Some of us would be satisfied by simply choosing deliverance from the eternal tormenting pits of hell and not continuing to seek greater wisdom and knowledge of His will. In other words, some have chosen fire insurance instead of seeking purity and that place of communion with Him. There are greater promises that we need to possess, but without knowledge of the will of God, those promises will never be inherited.

What can the Word do? The Word is able to cleanse when applied to the heart. When we decide to expose the hidden sins of our heart to the Faithful One, they will be forgiven, and light will immediately take over the darkness. Instantaneously, we will be cleansed from all our sin. Once the light dissipates the darkness, our intimacy with Him becomes unhindered and we are now able to stand righteously in His presence. Our life should be a pursuit of holiness. It is not a race to be run by ourselves and it is not by our own ability that we maintain clean hands and a pure heart. We gain that ability by acknowledging Jesus Christ as our personal Savior. When we pursue holiness by our ability we will surely fail. If we place our trust in the Word of God, it will wash and sanctify us as water removes dirt. I know the blood of Jesus Christ will remove the tainting of your past, and the Spirit of God will bring you to life from death, hope from hopelessness, and will empower you to run your new race with endurance.

He handpicked us to run the race on the winning team. There will be many times of weariness, but He is always there to gird us with His strength. We need to fix our eyes on the promise ahead and know that when we are weak, He is strong. The guarantee of His promise is stamped on our hearts, and we place our total trust and hope in that promise. The things of the world should become insignificant because our significance comes when we choose to tell others of His goodness, love, and mercy to those who are lost and dying. Telling and inviting them to have a personal relationship with Christ is the key because they need to experience the purity of life, cleanliness of spirit, and true love.

Nothing is sweeter than the intimacy of pure love. Many have never tasted it because we are trapped in a bed of lies, promises of love only to find superficial sex, used and rejected time and again while becoming ensnared by words of love from others. The trap of defiled love is endless. Our hearts have been deceived many times, but God longs to give us life and embrace us with His love.

All of us have a story to tell. Leah was alone in life, longing for freedom, and tormented by feelings of unworthiness. Voices lied, telling her she would never be good enough and never clean enough to stand in God's presence; she believed her life was too dirty for Him to love and accept her. The lies she believed about not deserving love kept her from knowing the pure love of God. Finally, realizing she had nothing to lose she turned her life over to the greatest love, and that love is now living in her, the Spirit of God. The keys to His throne room have been given, and she has access to the greatest wisdom anyone could impart.

Out there is a world of lost and dying people who are destined for death, hell and destruction. How will they know of the love of God and feel the indwelling of His Spirit and understand the gift of His Word unless we tell them? There is a need for them to understand that His love is so sweet, so pure, and it longs to satisfy their thirsty soul. A life that was once ensnared by hopelessness can now be set free. Does your heart cry out for freedom today? Will you declare your heart loyal to the One who created you, the One who loves you and pursues you? He longs for you to return to His hands and come home.

His passion is to show Himself strong on our behalf and to prove to us a love we've never known. It's an amazing thing! The God who is love, knows all, and is all-powerful is searching for those hearts; a heart that would say, "Yes!" All you have to do is believe that He sent His Son, Jesus Christ, to walk this earth, to die on the cross, and to rise again on the third day for you. He desires a heart that will invite His presence in. There are no other prerequisites and you are not required to clean yourself up first. All you need is a willing and loyal heart.

As we walk through life, we are sometimes rejected, most of the time judged and abused, and we don't measure up to the standards set by the world. Many of us often will feel unworthy, and it's difficult to comprehend that someone as great as God could love us. We may view God as being harsh and judgmental and automatically disqualify ourselves from drawing near to Him. Those who are worldly aren't aware that God disqualifies no one. We disqualify ourselves by willfully rejecting Him. We must realize every decision we make in life will yield consequences, good or bad. We can be led by our physical desires, the desires of our mind, will, and emotions to consequences either of life or destruction. When the Spirit of God lives in us, we are able to listen to the inner voice that always yields good consequences and leads us to abundant life. The Spirit of God is all-knowing and guides and directs our lives if we allow Him. We must always heed His voice and yield to His counsel. When we yield to the Spirit of God, the power from on high will bring life to every dead situation and circumstance in our life, taking us to the perfect will of God. When you are hopeless and feel unloved and unworthy, try Christ. He will be there to love you when no one else will; He will hold you when no one else would, and transform your life in a moment when everything else you have reached for can't.

After someone comes to Christ, it is important to continue this new walk alongside them. A person who has been saturated in sin for years does not recognize accountability. I found that out by mentoring Leah. It is difficult for the newly-saved to realize that living a life with Christ takes submission and commitment, but the accountability and submission needs to start with the mentor. It is the mentor's responsibility to hold those who are new in Christ close so that they don't roam back to the vices of the past; vices that can call loudly at times. Vices are the first thing they will try to run to because they are familiar. It takes commitment and patience to raise those from a life of sin into a new life in Christ. But the rewards are great! One thing you will learn through this process is how to walk in the love of Christ. I will tell you that keeping Leah close has been personally worth it to me; it has changed my focus, perception, and my life.

My words and advice to you are this: Reach out to someone who needs the Lord in their life. Step out of your personal agenda and help them find their one true love. I know for a fact this will stretch you at times and challenge you most of the time, but the rewards are great.

Many months before I met Leah, God spoke the following word to me: "I'm bringing them in by my Spirit, those whom the world can't offer freedom. They will come in for refuge—a safe place. I will bring deliverance to those who have longed for freedom. I don't see as the world sees, I see them as a mighty army. You are to embrace them, accept them and I will transform them. Then, more will come. The spirit of death will be on many. What has taken years in the past to free them will take moments. This will be a sign to the unbeliever, for the world has not seen this before. Don't be fooled by appearances. Those who are in the greatest bondage will not appear to be in bondage. Your harvest is in the harvest. Remember the coin in the mouth of the fish."

At the time God spoke this prophetic word to me, I was not aware of the journey I would face with Leah a mere seven months later. I never imagined that God would bring a woman into my life, who looked fine on the surface and acted like she didn't have a care in the world, but who was spiritually bound by death and hell. It was only after surrendering my own will in order to carry out the will of my Father—while learning how to adopt a heart like Him— that I truly realized what "the harvest is in the harvest" and "the coin is in the mouth of the fish" meant. Our "harvest" is in the souls that become saved; the "coin in the mouth of the fish" are blessings we receive because of our obedience to the call of the Father.

Now, if there is one thing in your life that can change everything, what would it be? Many would say money could effect much change! But after reaching out to Leah—who was so engulfed in sin and destined for hell—I can wholeheartedly answer in this way: The one thing that I found changed everything for me was my commitment to a tarnished treasure! Leading Leah to the Lord, mentoring her, walking her through the release of her bondage, and being a witness as God cleansed and polished her actually transformed *my* life!

When we seek after the things that are the heart of God— souls—then His favor will be released into our lives in all areas. Seeking the things of the natural is not the heart of God and will hinder the blessings and favor of God on our life. Oh, how glad I am that I listened to His voice and heeded His call! My life has changed in so many ways and I now know the true blessings of God.

IT'S TIME

For God so loved the world that He gave His only Son, that whosoever believes in Him will not die, but have eternal life.

John 3:16 (NKJV)

Do the lies and deception that you've harbored in your heart speak so loudly you think it's too late for change? Will the voices of your past tell you that you are too tainted and too used for God to love you? Or will you decide to be the one who makes up her mind to walk the path of life you were destined to walk. My prayer for anyone who seeks a new life in Christ is that a hedge of protection will seal and cover you from the voice of the enemy who speaks lies. I declare that the hopelessness, discouragement, shame, guilt and oppression will not keep you from obtaining your prize in finding Christ. I speak to the ones whom God has set on the path of mentoring the newly-saved to be strengthened and encouraged by your plan and purpose. I command every lying and tormenting spirit to be silenced so you will have ears to hear, eyes to see and a heart to obey. I pray the vision that is set in front of you can be seen with clarity and the force within can be felt. I declare every lie and every form of deceit that hinders you is broken. I speak a peace to your mind and boldness to your spirit man that will drive you to finish the plan and purpose God has given you. I declare to all women: You are free! Free to be the treasure that He has called you to be and free to see the gift He created you to be. I command the blinders of the lies of the enemy to be removed so you have eyes to see who you truly are.

Today, begin the pursuit of your promises and do not grow weary. Realize the source of power within you is not of yourself, but of the Spirit of God. Rely on Him and trust Him to lead you. You have the assurance that He will never leave you.

To those who have no personal relationship with Christ: Do not look to the failures of your past, because the past is the past and cannot be changed. It's over with and done. You need to look to your future. It's already been completed and planned out for you. If you walk in a life with Christ, you will never have to look back and have regrets. If you've never reached out your hand to dance with the Savior and submitted to the Savior as the Lord of your life, today He calls you by name to dance with Him. Will you reach out and say, "Yes"? Today is the day you can walk free. Pray the following prayer and know that when you do, your life will immediately be transformed from a tarnished treasure into the treasure you were meant to be.

God, I return to you this day

Take me by the hand

Reveal Your purpose within me

I trust You

Cleanse me of my past

I forgive myself

I need You more than life itself

I declare every form of evil no longer has authority over me

I give full authority to my Master

The One who was born named Jesus

The One who lived as a man and walked the earth

The One who suffered and died on the cross

The One who was buried and rose again on the third day

The One who sits at the right hand of God Almighty

This day I declare You are my Savior

I declare You are my deliverer

Set me on the path today of the greatest race ever

I will run it with endurance

I will not grow weary

I will not give up

My victory is in You, Jesus Christ

I am a child of the Master

I will finish the race and I will obtain the prize

In Jesus' name!

EPILOGUE

After many years in ministry, I finally realized there is only one way to draw a person into the kingdom of light who has been so hurt and so hardened by the world, and that is by love. Unconditional love is the God-kind of love that does not hold a person's past against them; but by teaching them that when we cry out to Him to be our Father, He will embrace them no matter how tainted and tarnished their past is. The battle to get Leah's life back to the Father's hands was over. She now lives under the shadow of the Almighty and finds her way in a safe place. It's a place she had never known in the world she lived in, all she knew was hurt and pain. She never knew such love and wondered her whole life if it was possible. It was possible and it is possible for you, too! There is a way out of the prison of hopelessness and pain. Know there is a God who is waiting with open arms to take you in and embrace you. There is a life waiting for you that will fulfill every need and longing you've ever had. Just like Leah, you can walk to your place of freedom and be able to take others to the same place of safety and love.